JENSEN

White River Valley Electric Cooperative

A Touchstone Energy® Cooperative

WHITE RIVER VALLEY ELEC.
CO-OP.
REA
HOLLISTER, MO.
No13

HIGH TECH AMONG THE HILLS

A HISTORY OF WHITE RIVER VALLEY ELECTRIC COOPERATIVE

by Pat Swinger

The Donning Company Publishers
184 Business Park Drive, Suite 206
Virginia Beach, VA 23462

Steve Mull, General Manager
Barbara Buchanan, Office Manager
Anne Burns, Editor
Tonya Washam, Graphic Designer
Priscilla Odango, Imaging Artist
Tonya Washam, Marketing Specialist
Pamela Engelhard, Marketing Advisor

John Richardson, Project Director

Library of Congress Cataloging-in-Publication Data

Swinger, Pat, 1951-
High tech among the hills : a history of White River Valley Electric Cooperative / by Pat Swinger.
p. cm.
ISBN 978-1-57864-676-0
1. White River Valley Electric Cooperative--History. 2. Electric utilities--Missouri--History. 3. Cooperative societies--Missouri--History. I. White River Valley Electric Cooperative. II. Title.
HD9685.U7W52 2011
334'.6813337932097787--dc22
2011005623
Printed in the United States of America at Walsworth Publishing Company

Table of Contents

National Rural Utilities
Cooperative Finance Corporation

2201 Cooperative Way
Herndon, Virginia 20171-3025
703-709-6700 | www.nrucfc.coop

A Touchstone Energy® Cooperative

March 3, 2011

Christopher Hamon, CEO
White River Valley Electric Cooperative
P.O. Box 969
Branson, MO 65616

Dear Chris:

I am writing to congratulate WRVEC on its long history of outstanding service. Through the years—from when the first switch was thrown to bring light to the valley, to when the cooperative's new headquarters building opened its doors this year—WRVEC has done an exceptional job of serving it members.

Electricity came to the White River Valley in 1939, and White River Valley Electric Cooperative has been committed to keeping the lights on ever since. Over its more than 70-year history, the cooperative has grown from serving 500 members to more than 48,000 across five counties in the Missouri Ozarks.

WRVEC is part of an American success story that has been too quickly and too often forgotten. Along with the more than 900 electric cooperatives spanning the country, WRVEC is providing an invaluable service to its members in areas once neglected by other electric utilities. By bringing affordable and reliable electricity to rural communities, these electric cooperatives have empowered rural people, fostered development and improved the rural quality of life in ways that would otherwise have been impossible.

Among electric cooperatives, WRVEC stands out with its strong record of growth and success. This record makes me confident that WRVEC will continue to flourish to the benefit of the communities it serves for generations to come.

As a $20 billion national financial cooperative devoted specifically to assisting America's electric cooperatives, CFC is proud to be a dedicated partner of WRVEC. CFC compliments WRVEC for your outstanding record of service to your members. We look forward to your continued success and we pledge that we will do our utmost to serve you in the decades ahead.

Cooperatively Yours,

Sheldon

Sheldon C. Petersen
Governor and Chief Executive Officer

Foreword

Our cooperative has a rich history, filled with over seventy-two years of colorful characters and stories of perseverance. As we move into the next generation of electric service, it is important for us to remember our roots and the incredible journey that has defined White River Valley Electric Cooperative.

I am proud to say that I have spent most of my adult life employed at WRVEC and have served as the CEO for the last twelve years. During my tenure I have learned we are very fortunate to call the Ozarks home as the same cooperative spirit that guided our founding members is still going strong and shaping the communities around us.

I want to share one of my favorite quotes about electrifying rural America with you as it embodies the story of WRVEC. Franklin D. Roosevelt said the following, "I think that the forward march of the electric cooperatives has an even more profound significance in terms of our fight to preserve democracy. For it represents what is perhaps the most democratic form of business enterprise, one in which the individual finds his greatest gain through cooperation with his neighbor."

I hope you enjoy this book, which was compiled with the help of many people who have had an impact on WRVEC, both in the past and the present. We did our best to include as many people and stories as possible, but there simply were not enough pages to include all the anecdotes that were uncovered while researching for this book.

It has been a great pleasure serving you for the last twenty-three years and I look forward to many more.

Chris Hamon, PE
CEO

Acknowledgments

We would like to thank the following people who, in true White River spirit, helped us gather the information, photos, and personal anecdotes that went into the production of this book.

Kenny Bilyeu
Ted Bookout
Myrtle Booth
Alta Mae Cary
Bill Davis
Larry Frazier
Oliver Gentry
Roy Grady
Chris Hamon
Carl and Emma Lou Hunt
Jeri Layton
Delbert Moore
Layne Morrill
Jeff Pardeck
Amy Rosier
Gary Soutee
Mark Speight
Dobie Youngblood

Introduction

White River Valley Electric Cooperative (WRVEC) has been serving the people of this five-county area since the first lines were electrified in 1939. In the seventy-two years since the first switch was flipped, so many changes have taken place that the current operation bears little resemblance to those earliest days. The landscape has changed as super highways have replaced ridgetop roads. The descendants of the Ozark pioneers now share the hills and hollers with pioneers of another kind—those who escaped the city to recreate their lives in the rural and recreational atmosphere of the White River Valley.

One thing, however, has remained constant—the dedication to the consumers, the members of White River Valley Electric Cooperative. Whether reading the words of its founders or talking to those who currently make up the White River team, one hears repeatedly the same sense of mission, deeply embedded in their White River roots, to improve the lives and lifestyles of everyone they serve. Whether you are talking to them about outages, the future cost of electricity, or the co-op's role in the community, the same phrase crops up time and again—"It's all about the members." It is a responsibility they are honored to bear.

Over the years, we have traded our agrarian lifestyle for the technology of the modern world. And while the service White River supplies has become virtually as necessary to our existence as the air we breathe, ironically we have come to take it for granted, a luxury afforded to us by the people of WRVEC.

Frank Dawes, who was the first president of the co-op and became its first manager in 1941, once wrote an article for the *Hill and Holler News* chronicling its formation. In it, he urged those of us who've known only the life of ease that electricity affords us to recall a harsher and more difficult time. "Don't forget the job we had to do," he wrote, "to convince your fathers and mothers that they could change from the backwoods life into a modern life. And don't forget the good old souls now departed that were so conservative they almost had to be driven to the use of electricity that most of you young folks and transplanted city folks take for granted today. When you go about your daily routine, with electricity a part of everything you do, we hope you will give a thought, once in a while, to how you happened to have it."

Heeding his advice, this book is about the men and women of White River Valley Electric Cooperative—their mission, their challenges, and their triumphs.

Chapter One
Life in the White River Valley

"Life used to be what you could scratch out of these rocks. Most folks didn't live—they just existed."

H. C. Gramke, Reeds Spring

White River Township was formed in 1833, an area divided off of Greene County which itself became Taney County in 1837. Over the years, Taney County was then whittled down to more manageable entities: Ozark County was established in 1841, Stone County in 1851, Christian County in 1859, and Douglas County in 1864, leaving Taney County as it is now.

Life on the farm was hard work from sunup to sundown and far from romantic. The evening meal was usually leftovers from the more important noon meal. Photo courtesy of Rural Missouri.

The earliest settlers came to this area from Tennessee, Kentucky, and the Carolinas. Most were of Scottish, English, and Irish heritage with an ingrained ability to survive the hills and crags of the Ozarks and scratch out survival from the thin, rocky soil. Settlers raised what crops they could to feed their families and bartered for supplies with their neighbors.

People from all over started coming to the Branson area after Harold Bell Wright's *The Shepherd of the Hills* was published in 1907. In the 1920s and 1930s, folks came from the cities by train to see Marvel Cave and Old

Matt's Cabin and taste the down-to-earth simplicity depicted in the famous book. But, these were the Dirty Thirties, as the decade came to be known, and life among the hills was anything but idyllic. The Great Depression continued to grip the nation; farmers suffered from falling crop prices and several years of drought in the mid-1930s drove many from their farms and homes.

Farm life, even into the 1930s, meant chores from sunrise to sundown, and life expectancy meant that few people saw their sixtieth birthday. Without proper hygiene and medical care, adults and children alike died of diseases that are now virtually

Getting a field ready for crops meant backbreaking days spent behind the horse and plow. Photo courtesy of Rural Missouri.

unknown. The lack of refrigeration led to food-borne illnesses. What machines they did have were either gas or steam-powered with dangerous blades, belts, or auger bits and accidents were often fatal if not debilitating. With no means for providing them warmth, livestock was often lost to the cold during winter.

Work in the field started early but before it could begin, horses had to be fed and harnessed, and cows needed milking. Upon return from the fields, many of these chores had to be done again before sundown. Harnesses needed repairing and a supply of wood had to be put up for the next day. Besides tending their homes, women had to help haul water, gather eggs from the henhouse, and tend the garden.

Most of their clothing was made by hand and women often used feed and flour sacks to make shirts and dresses. Manufacturers eager to sell their products obliged them by packaging the flour and feed in pretty floral prints. They learned early to bake their own bread, make their own soap, and preserve everything from beef and pork to the produce grown in their backyard gardens, spending hours over a wood stove during the hot summer months.

Norwood Speight, who would go on to become manager of White River Valley Electric Co-op for almost thirty years, recalled life before electricity. "I grew up in a home without any electricity whatsoever—in the house or the barn or anywhere." He spoke of sitting down to the table with a kerosene lamp to read by, conscious of the fact that the slightest breeze meant a nearby curtain might catch fire. He spoke of the family's cellar where they stored fruits and vegetables in order to have edible food during the winter. Hardier produce like turnips, carrots, and apples were buried to preserve them. He remembered hog killing time, salting down the meat to preserve it and rendering the fat for soap making. His

Late fall was usually hog butchering time and without refrigeration, people shared both the work and the meat.

We lived on a little ridge farm just south of Kirbyville in Taney County. There were three children—I was about nine years old—and we had a well that didn't even give enough for drinking water. So on washday, my father would take the big black kettle, the washtubs and the washboard and haul them about a half a mile down to the big spring. My mother would gather her clothes together, fix a lunch, and take the soap that she needed and dad would take us all down to the big spring in the wagon. He'd go ahead with his plowing in the fields nearby and before he went he'd build a big fire under the kettle and it was my job to keep wood under it. The big kettle was filled and the washtub and washboard were set up under the shade of a pin oak tree and clotheslines were strung among the tree branches. Mother would start the washing. She'd wash the white clothes first and then by that time it was probably noon and she would fix a little lunch for us over the fire, spread a little tablecloth and Dad would come in from the field and we'd have our lunch together. —Douglas Mahnkey

greatest sympathy, however, was directed at the women of White River country. "Clothes had to be washed and they had to be dried some way and about the only way we knew of was just to hang them out and let them dry. Imagine frozen shirts and pants and socks on the line!"

Douglas Mahnkey, White River attorney and historian, recalled washday for his family. Being a child at the time, the day held a great deal more magic for him than it might have for his parents.

Mr. H. C. Gramke of Reeds Spring knew all too well how difficult life could be in the Ozarks before electricity. "Life used to be what you could scratch out of these rocks. Most folks didn't live—they just existed. We were near a power

Washday was an arduous task and whenever possible, women helped each other hauling water and keeping the wood fires burning. Photo courtesy of Rural Missouri.

company line—but they weren't interested in us when we asked for service."

Women needed two flat irons, also known as sad irons—one to press with while the other reheated on the wood stove. Photo courtesy of Rural Missouri.

Ted Bookout, who would later collect stories like these from White River's members for the *Hill and Holler News*, had his own recollections of life before electricity. Born in a log cabin in 1931 on land his grandparents had homesteaded, Ted's family lived about four miles north of Branson. With no automobile they relied on a horse and wagon to get to town to purchase feed and supplies. "I remember my dad keeping records of his chickens. I think he made $600 on the farm one year. My mom worked in a laundry and I can remember her walking to town on the old gravel road. People were determined to make a living one way or another. You were happy if you found a job."

Ted's older siblings later told him a story about their father's efforts to scratch out a living for his family during the Depression. They remembered their father cutting a wagonload of wood with an old crosscut saw. He loaded it into the wagon

The noon meal was often taken out in the field to save the farmers valuable daylight.

and took it in to town to sell it. Later that day he came back with the same load of wood, unable to sell any of it.

Help for the American farmer was on the way as the Depression softened in the mid-1930s. Philosophical differences broiled in Congress as legislators wrestled with the issue of how much help Uncle Sam should be expected to extend and to what degree people should be expected to "pull themselves up by their own bootstraps." The reformers among Congress won out and in 1935 a second round of New Deal legislation was enacted. However, this time the legislation was geared less on relief and more on creating avenues for sustainable change. The Resettlement Administration (RA) was formed as a land resource management agency moving farmers from subsistence land to more fertile ground. In some areas, suburban developments sprang up for resettlement of displaced farmers. By 1937 the RA was reorganized under the Agriculture Department as the Farm Security Administration and redirected its resources toward offering loans, grants, and agricultural education.

How many of these programs reached the Ozark hills, it's hard to say. And while Missouri farmers weren't directly impacted by passage of the Tennessee Valley Act in 1933, it certainly helped to shed light on the problems they faced. TVA authorized the construction of a dam, later named Norris Dam for the Nebraska senator, intended to provide farmers relief from depleted soil and periodic flooding. But the most dramatic change for farmers would come from the electricity generated by TVA dams.

Chapter Two
Let There Be Light

A good wife laughs at her husband's jokes, not because they are clever, but because she is.

Excerpt from "Grandpa Sez" in the* White River Co-op News, *1960s.

The White River Valley wasn't a total stranger to electricity. The Empire District Electric Company, based in Joplin, was incorporated in 1909. The New York financiers who invested in the company referred to the region as "Little Empire" as a way of expressing their pride for their home state known as the Empire State. Soon thereafter, Empire built the Powersite Dam near Forsyth, Missouri, creating Lake Taneycomo and drawing tourists to nearby communities Branson and Rockaway Beach. Even before the Depression hit, the old English Village was built in the little town of Hollister providing a quaint and charming respite for tourists.

Before the poles and lines could go up, the right-of-way had to be cleared.

The Empire District Electric Company served the more populated towns in the region—Reeds Spring, Forsyth, Branson, and Hollister—but the investor-owned company wasn't interested in serving the rural areas. In the 1930s, the prevailing notion was that providing power to the remote rural areas wasn't economically feasible. The more densely populated cities used a 2,300-volt distribution system that could only extend about four miles before the voltage drop became unacceptable. When commercial power companies did provide power to the outlying areas, they charged as much as seven cents per kilowatt-hour at a time when laborer's wages were only twenty-five cents per hour.

President Roosevelt signed Executive Order No. 7037 on May 11, 1935, creating the Rural Electrification Administration. *Photo courtesy of* Rural Missouri.

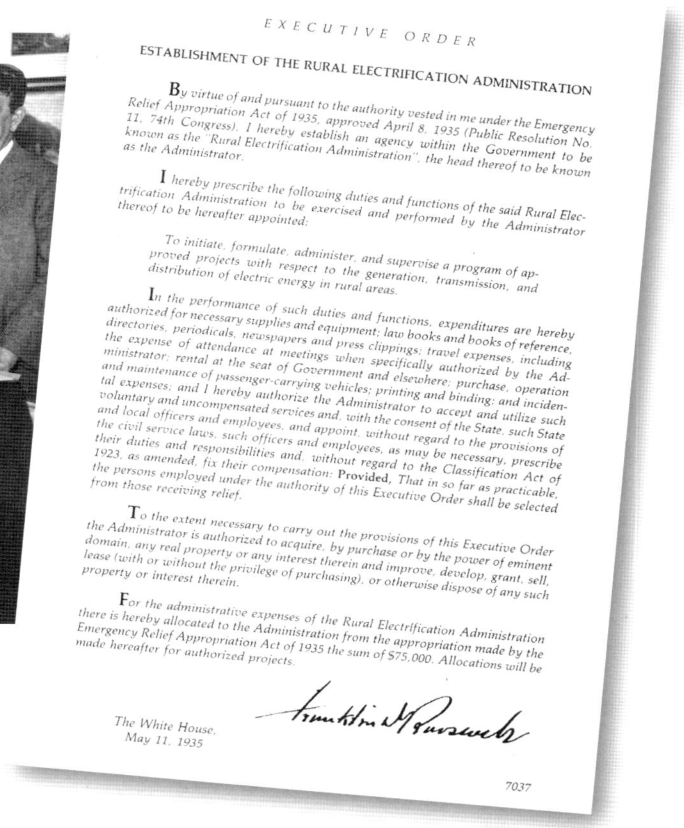

E X E C U T I V E   O R D E R

ESTABLISHMENT OF THE RURAL ELECTRIFICATION ADMINISTRATION

By virtue of and pursuant to the authority vested in me under the Emergency Relief Appropriation Act of 1935, approved April 8, 1935 (Public Resolution No. 11, 74th Congress), I hereby establish an agency within the Government to be known as the "Rural Electrification Administration", the head thereof to be known as the Administrator.

I hereby prescribe the following duties and functions of the said Rural Electrification Administration to be exercised and performed by the Administrator thereof to be hereafter appointed:

To initiate, formulate, administer, and supervise a program of approved projects with respect to the generation, transmission, and distribution of electric energy in rural areas.

In the performance of such duties and functions, expenditures are hereby authorized for necessary supplies and equipment; law books and books of reference, directories, periodicals, newspapers and press clippings; travel expenses, including the expense of attendance at meetings when specifically authorized by the Administrator; rental at the seat of Government and elsewhere; purchase, operation and maintenance of passenger-carrying vehicles; printing and binding; and incidental expenses; and I hereby authorize the Administrator to accept and utilize such voluntary and uncompensated services and, with the consent of the State, such State and local officers and employees, and appoint, without regard to the provisions of the civil service laws, such officers and employees, as may be necessary, prescribe their duties and responsibilities and, without regard to the Classification Act of 1923, as amended, fix their compensation: **Provided,** *That in so far as practicable, the persons employed under the authority of this Executive Order shall be selected from those receiving relief.*

To the extent necessary to carry out the provisions of this Executive Order the Administrator is authorized to acquire, by purchase or by the power of eminent domain, any real property or any interest therein and improve, develop, grant, sell, lease (with or without the privilege of purchasing), or otherwise dispose of any such property or interest therein.

For the administrative expenses of the Rural Electrification Administration there is hereby allocated to the Administration from the appropriation made by the Emergency Relief Appropriation Act of 1935 the sum of $75,000. Allocations will be made hereafter for authorized projects.

The White House,
May 11, 1935

7037

Photo courtesy of Rural Missouri.

Doug Mahnkey recalled life near Forsyth where he and his wife lived. "The private power company served Forsyth but they didn't want to build lines outside the town. We even suggested that we would put up $500 of our own the money for the lines out to our place if they would build them. But we couldn't get it done." When he was interviewed for a radio program in the 1980s, Doug elaborated: "When they (Empire) built the dam at Ozark Power, Forsyth was a mile away and had ninety-one inhabitants but they didn't want to serve Forsyth. Power companies had the idea that the only way to be profitable was to be in the larger population centers. So Joplin, Springfield and those places were going to get the power rather than the people who lived right by the dam."

Those who could afford it sometimes took matters into their own hands, and so it was in Forsyth. As Doug explained, "A group of interested citizens in Forsyth formed a private corporation—I believe it was called the Forsyth Electric Company—and they put up the poles the mile up to the dam and bought the power from the Ozark Power Company and served Forsyth. Later they sold out to the company."

Little did they know, this do-it-yourself attitude was to be duplicated on a much larger scale. They were on the verge of witnessing, and helping to create, a radical change in the rural American landscape.

Frank Dawes, pictured here in 1961, was White River's first board president, first construction superintendent, and first manager.

The Rural Electrification Administration

Traditionally, co-ops have sprung up in America whenever the marketplace fails to provide necessary goods or services at affordable prices, and in the case of rural electric cooperatives, both the market and the timing were just right.

Continuing on the reforms initiated through the second wave of New Deal legislation, President Franklin Delano Roosevelt issued executive order No. 7037 creating the Rural Electrification Administration on May 11, 1935, under authority of the Emergency Relief Appropriation Act of 1935. Representative John E. Rankin of Mississippi and Senator George William Norris of Nebraska, two members of Congress who, though they were on either end of the political spectrum, were united in their concern for the lives of rural Americans, proposed the idea for the REA. Senator Norris later became known as the Father of the Tennessee Valley Authority. The following year, Congress passed the Norris-Rayburn Act appropriating $410 million for a ten-year program.

The Rural Electrification Administration was part of a relief package designed to stimulate the rural economies by bringing them into the modern era. Electricity would improve the lives of rural farmers and provide them with the means to increase their productivity. It reflected Roosevelt's belief that people were better off being given, as they now say, a hand up instead of a hand out. Only two restrictions were placed on the cooperatives: they would not be allowed to compete directly with investor-owned utility companies and

This one-room rural school at Walnut Shade was built in 1896 and served the community's schoolchildren until 1953. Area residents met in this building one night in 1940 and learned of the new White River Electric Cooperative, which was soon to extend the first electric service to the community.

Wiley A. Floyd

Wiley A. Floyd owned a general store at Bradleyville in the late 1930s and was one of the early organizers who met in February 1939. He began working in his area, recruiting members to sign up for electricity. "I guess I must have driven four or five thousand miles, over all kinds of roads signing up members," he recalled. He only had one person turn him down though a few times he personally loaned prospective members the $5.00 for the membership fee. Only once was he not paid back.

Mr. Floyd served on the cooperative board until February of 1941 and continued to operate his store until the early 1950s, taking great delight in the electric lighting and refrigeration.

W. A. Floyd, pictured here in 1971, was one of the original incorporators of White River Valley Electric Cooperative.

no one living in a city with a population of 1,500 or more could be a co-op member.

In an interview given years later, Norwood Speight, manager of White River from 1946 to 1975, confirmed the government's intentions: "The interest rate to be charged on those funds at that time was 2% because 2% was what the money actually cost the government and the government

Goldie Howard, lineman. The REA logo on the truck shows the importance of the REA to rural folks.

The Hollister crew, left to right: Wayne McFarland, Frank Davis, and Austin Brittain.

was not to make any profit out of this. The 2% would be sufficient to cover the administrative costs on top of the actual costs. Never did the government have any idea of giving anything to the rural people. They wanted the rural people to have an opportunity to pay for their electric service."

Early Meetings

Now came the difficult task of organizing this group of independent, self-reliant, and naturally skeptical people. One of those facing the task was Frank Dawes, a man who later became a construction superintendent for the co-op. He was elected the first president of the co-op at the incorporator's meeting on February 6, 1939, and was its first

Supplies were hard to come by during WWII, but the men of White River were ready to go to work.

Pete Klineline with a new one-ton International truck, July 1949.

manager from 1941 to 1946. Frank related the story of White River's organization in the April 1961 newsletter, giving a detailed description of those early days:

Back in the winter of 1938-39, a notice appeared in the White River Leader, then ably edited and published by Evelyn and Forest Runyon, that a representative from REA in Washington was going to be in Branson to talk to a group of residents of Taney County that were interested in the development of rural electricity for the area. The meeting was held in the Christian Church and was attended by about fifty people. Since we had not been numbered among the original group that caused this meeting to be held, we sat quietly in the rear of the meeting place to see what would happen. The speaker, Joseph McCombs, a southerner with an unmistakable Georgia drawl, began to unfold the prospects. Although Joe did not talk like an Ozarkian, he kindled the fire in the hearts of enough people that an organization was set up and a Board of Directors was selected by random suggestions of names by those present at the meeting.

According to Frank, the process got bogged down by a few people who were "looking out for their own self interests," people with axes to grind and who were generally cynical. Unable to sign up the necessary number of farmers, the effort came to a halt.

Then, during the summer of 1939, another attempt was made. With a different group of people spearheading the project, things went much better. Once again, they made their pitch to the rural schools, the churches, the women's clubs, and the leaders of the various rural communities, as well as the *White*

J. C. "Uncle Johnny" Harlin

One of the first directors of the WRVEC was J. C. Harlin, known to his friends as "Uncle Johnny." He served as the co-op's first vice president from 1939 to 1941, president from 1941 to 1945, and then as a board member from 1945 to 1949 when he resigned. When the Gainesville electric plant became inoperative in 1940, Mr. Harlin was instrumental in getting the co-op electric line extended from Kissee Mills to Gainesville in the incredibly short period of thirty days.

The president of the Bank of Gainesville since 1908, J. C.'s public service extended far beyond the electric cooperative. In Ozark County, he served as collector for thirty-six years, county clerk for eight years, and treasurer for four years. He was state senator from 1930 to 1934 during which time he was instrumental in establishing the Missouri State Highway Patrol and co-authored the Missouri school bus law of 1931, which provided for the safe transportation of school children. He was a member of the State Highway Commission from 1947 to 1954 and was serving as state representative from Ozark County at the time of his death. Described as the "most beloved citizen of Ozark County," J. C. Harlin passed away on December 18, 1955.

River Leader. They laid out a plan for the first portions of the system, all on highways that extended on Highway 65 from the Arkansas line to Highlandville, as well as from old Forsyth up to Chadwick.

Frank Dawes recalled walking many miles that spring, obtaining legal easements from landowners allowing the cooperative to place poles on their land. While trying to spread the good news of the coming modern miracle of electricity, Frank wrote that he was "rebuffed by some, laughed at by others and once even shot at."

Doug Mahnkey had his own recollections of those early meetings: "We'd hold schoolhouse meetings and advertise them in the local press. We'd have good crowds and a lot of good questions were asked. I remember attending a meeting up in Christian County. Ed Bowles, one of the organizers of the co-op, was the instigator of the meeting. Mrs. Mahnkey and I and her parents drove up there—it was a bad cold night in January. People were asked to put up the five dollars and sign an application blank to get enough people involved that we could form the corporation."

Less than 25 percent of the area landowners signed up. Some of the farmers told Frank the only reason they didn't come to the meeting in Forsyth was simply that they hadn't been off their farm, for any purpose, for thirty years. Many people promised to hook on to the lines as their construction neared their own properties but were unwilling to put up the $5.00 membership fee in advance. As Frank told it, others who refused to sign up told them, "Pappy got along without electricity, so why should we change his ways," or "That juice will run right down them wires and kill all them kids in the house," that "they had a good spring in which to keep their milk and butter and didn't need a new-fangled refrigerator."

Floodwaters of Lake Taneycomo reached the White River office in Hollister in May of 1950.

Norwood Speight witnessed those concerns firsthand. "Rural people were fearful that the lines would fall down and burn up their farms and their homes," he said. "In Dade County where I grew up, some of the lines were torn down and some of the wire stolen because some of the people were afraid of electricity."

Norwood Speight's picture appeared regularly in the Hill and Holler News.

They finally won over the farmers, but there were still obstacles to overcome. Though they'd signed up six hundred prospective users, economics experts in Washington, D.C., decided since the average cash income of the farmers in that area was only $400 a year, the area could not support an electric system and bureaucrats in Washington weren't inclined to make loans that couldn't be paid back. Frank Dawes recalled, "It was only after we had been able to prove that the cash income of an Ozarker was only a part of his independent living, that we were able to get an allotment of funds for the building of those first two hundred miles."

The White River Valley Electric Cooperative

The articles of incorporation of the White River Valley Electric Cooperative were signed on February 6, 1939. The names of the original incorporators were as follows:

M. P. Pierce of Forsyth
W. L. Humphrey of Forsyth
Arch Madden of Branson
Hazel Powell Tyson of Reeds Spring
Alice Markham of Reeds Spring
Grant Stennett of Garrison
Ed Bowles of Chadwick
J. C. Brand of Forsyth
Hobart Parnell of Walnut Shade
Jesse Wright of Taneyville
A. D. McDonald of Gainesville
W. A. Floyd of Bradleyville
F. A. Dawes of Hollister
J. C. Harlin of Gainesville

Miss Minnee Ranslow, age eighty-four, was featured in the August 1955 newsletter having just received electricity at her farm near Taneyville. Echoing the sentiments of many others she said, "I have always been afraid of it and didn't think I could afford it."

These organizers met in the basement of the Christian Church in Branson back in 1939. They then moved the meetings to the Security Bank in Branson and the Hollister post office. Frank Dawes was hired as the co-op's first manager and the first office was finally rented on Front Street, now Downing Street, in Hollister. Believing they needed an attorney from the Branson area, Henry Awbery was hired until about 1945 when he passed away. Robert L. Gideon and Doug Mahnkey were then chosen to represent the co-op. Doug remained with them until December of 1978.

The city of Hollister was vulnerable to frequent flooding from Lake Taneycomo in the days before Table Rock Dam. Alta Mae Cary recalled the flood in May of 1950 that dumped approximately eighteen inches of water in the Hollister office. "They packed up their office equipment and file cabinets and carried them up the hill to our Presbyterian Church and opened up the office in the basement of the church."

In 1939 the REA was reorganized as a division of the U.S. Department of Agriculture. The first REA loan to White River was approved on March 20, 1940, and the first 195-mile section of line was built and energized by September 4, 1940. Two hundred and sixty-four members received electricity for the first time.

Setting poles and stringing electrical lines were new for these men of White River as it was for most men in the rural areas across the country. To help out, the REA drafted plans and set engineering standards. To make the funding reach

First Accounts

Account No. 1 on the line built north from the Forsyth substation to Highlandville belonged to Mr. and Mrs. Jerry Brown who lived just north of old Highway 65 on Highway 160. They received their electric service on September 11, 1940. Their first appliance was a radio they purchased to listen to the music of Roy Acuff who later earned the nickname "King of Country Music."

Mr. I. N. "Newt" Bilyeu, who lived just south of Spokane, was the second account and the third was credited to Mr. Carl F. Aehle at the former location of the Spokane post office and grocery store.

Account No. 4 went to Mr. and Mrs. Earl Bilyeu who lived about one mile north of Spokane. The Bilyeu's operated a tomato-canning factory from 1920 to 1950 and remember well the day the electricity came on. "We were busy in the tomato cannery and had a lady sitting with our small children," Mrs. Bilyeu recalled in a June 1966 interview. "All at once she burst through the door with a child in her arms screaming, 'The lights are on! The lights are on!'"

The 1951 annual meeting.

as far as possible, the REA saw to it that the specifications were as economical as possible. Materials were standardized to provide economies of scale for the materials suppliers.

REA crews traveled through the American countryside installing wiring in houses and barns. A standard REA installation in a house consisted of a 60-amp, 230-volt fuse panel with a 60-amp range circuit, a 20-amp kitchen circuit, and two or three 15-amp lighting circuits. A ceiling-mounted light fixture was installed in each room, controlled either by a pull chain or a single switch mounted near a door. Electrical appliances were few so, at most, one outlet was installed in each room.

Lights On!

Many White River members recalled their lives before and after electricity in the *Hill and Holler News*. Mr. and Mrs. James Davis became White River's Account No. 24 when they received electricity at their farm about four miles southwest of Spokane in Christian County on August 15, 1940. They installed a 120-volt service with a 30-ampere meter loop, which was "plenty" of electric capacity for those days. It cost the Davis's less than $25.00 to wire their home. Mr. Davis helped to build the electric lines back then, as did so many other members. He helped to dig pole holes and furnished a team of horses to haul poles into place. Mrs. Davis said, "Our first appliances were an electric radio (our first) and a wringer washer. Today (1973) I have an automatic washer and I am going to get an electric clothes dryer."

Account No. 46 was Mr. and Mrs. Ralph Gideon who received electricity at their home in Riverside late in the summer of 1940. They'd had their house wired in anticipation and when the line was energized, they looked forward to nightfall so they could use their lights. "We also changed from an ice box to an electric refrigerator right away, and that was something wonderful!" Mr. Gideon said. Mrs. Gideon reflected, "To us, the news that electricity was going to be available in the rural countryside seemed like a dream. It didn't seem possible we could have it."

Delbert Moore, a White River employee for over forty years, remembered how eager people were to join the co-op, particularly after they heard their neighbors tell of laborsaving appliances. "They'd be out in the yard just waiting for the meter to start moving."

Carl Hunt, a White River lineman, was originally from Jefferson County. But his wife, Emma Lou, lived in the tiny town of Dawt when her family got electricity. "I remember the day we got it," she said. "I went to grade school and my dad had bought a refrigerator and an electric iron. I came in and my mom was ironing with this electric iron. And cold milk! It was great. I remember the very day."

White River Valley Electric Cooperative, Incorporated

Organized Under the Laws of Missouri

CERTIFICATE Nº 4021

Membership Certificate

THIS CERTIFIES THAT a membership in WHITE RIVER VALLEY ELECTRIC COOPERATIVE, Incorporated, (hereinafter called the "Cooperative") is held by R. F. Hammon, Hollister, Missouri

This Certificate and the membership evidenced hereby are not transferable except as provided by the by-laws of the Cooperative, and such membership may be terminated as provided in said by-laws. Upon termination of the membership represented by this certificate, by death, cessation of existence, expulsion or withdrawal, this certificate shall be surrendered to the Cooperative. Each member of the Cooperative, or in the case of a joint membership, the holders thereof jointly, or either of them, but not both shall be entitled to One (1) Vote and no more upon each matter submitted to a vote at all meetings of the members of the Cooperative.

This certificate and the membership evidenced hereby are subject to all the terms, conditions, and limitations contained in the Charter and By-laws of the Cooperative and all amendments thereto and in the application of the holder or holders hereof for membership in the Cooperative.

IN WITNESS WHEREOF the Cooperative has caused this certificate to be signed by its President and Secretary and its corporate seal to be hereunto affixed this 30th day of July, 1949.

(CORPORATE SEAL)

President.

Secretary.

THE ROSEBUD NEWS, ROSEBUD, TEXAS

Robert Hamon's membership certificate dated July 30, 1949.

Mr. H. C. Gramke of Reeds Spring knew how difficult life was in the Ozarks before electricity and though they lived near a power company line, they were refused when they asked for service. "Then the REC's (rural electric cooperatives) started up and we learned how to live," he said. "We got into the cedar furniture business with our own cedar and power tools using co-op electricity. Life has been good to us since then. We were able to modernize our home and even put in a bathroom."

Mrs. A. D. McDonald operated a general store in Gainesville with her husband from 1923 to 1956. Prior to receiving electricity in September of 1940, power was supplied by a small generator in town that was turned off at midnight and turned on at six a.m. each morning. Before becoming White River's Account No. 90, they bought ice for cooling "pop" but didn't have any way to keep fresh produce, meats, milk, or ice cream. Said Mrs. McDonald, "Our customers probably enjoyed our updated store as much as we did. I think we appreciated having a pump in our well and running water in the house as much as anything."

The rear of White River's office, next to Ye English Inn in Hollister, 1949.

Most homes had only one light bulb in the center of the room and each room had only one outlet, most frequently reserved for the radio. In the hot summer months, it was sometimes used for a fan, which was, of course, hauled into the bedroom at the end of the day to make sleeping a little easier. Remembering those days, Alta Mae Cary said, "A fan was a real luxury...a real treat." While the refrigerator was usually the wife's first request, most men were eager for an outdoor yard light to replace the kerosene lantern they carried out to the barn to check on the livestock.

Many families continued to see the lights go on for the first time in the early 1950s, among them Ted Bookout's parents. His mother wrote him a letter when they got electricity to tell him she'd purchased a Betty Crocker electric iron. Alta Mae remembered her father, Robert Hamon's, continued efforts to bring electricity to Pine Top. "He got out and walked to all of his neighboring farmers and told them about the membership. Five dollars back then was a lot of money. He told people about White River and what they would do and the electricity was through Kirbyville and that's where they had to start. A lot of farmers wanted the help of electricity mostly to pump water but some of them just didn't have the five dollars." Alta Mae was working away from home when her parents finally got electricity at their home in Pine Top. They didn't even have running water yet and her mother had a washing machine with a gasoline motor on it.

White River's Christmas party, 1952.

But Alta Mae's mother found something else to get excited about. "My mother was very fond of jello but she didn't have a refrigerator. My brother was there and when the lights came on Mother said, 'Well, good! Now I can make jello.'"

Doug Mahnkey, when interviewed with Norwood Speight years ago, reminded everyone of the skepticism that challenged the wisdom of bringing electricity to the simple folks who lived among the hills and hollers. "A lot of people were skeptical," he said. "They said farmers wouldn't use electricity, but time has proved them so wrong. As everyone knows, farmers now use electricity to grind their feed, to pump their water, to heat the water for their livestock—just thousands of uses of electricity. So everyone was so dead wrong about the farmers and rural people using electricity."

Source used in chapter: http://www.coopmonth.coop/download_files/economicimpact.final.pdf\

Chapter Three
The First Steps of an Uphill Climb

"If it hadn't been for the New Deal...you wouldn't have these dams. Put that in your pipe and smoke it."

President Harry Truman at the dedication of Bull Shoals Dam

In 1940 the only electric transmission and distribution in Ozark County came from a small plant in Gainesville. Residents received little power, only having access to electricity between 4 p.m. and 8 a.m., and paid an excessive rate for it. The plant broke down in 1940 and WRVEC was asked to build lines to Gainesville.

Due to the urgency of the situation, the board agreed to build a line from Kissee Mills to Gainesville. Poles and materials scheduled to be used on other construction sites were moved to the Gainesville job.

Every opportunity was taken to broadcast the benefits of electricity.

A Lot to Learn

Beyond their single lightbulb rooms, people weren't sure at first what use they might have for their newly acquired electricity. According to Frank Dawes, another challenge was helping people understand the minimum bill of $2.70 did not mean that was to be their maximum usage. "We had a terrific tug-of-war to get them to use more than the $2.70 minimum bill each month," he said. Co-op leaders tried to convince the local hardware and furniture stores to stock electrical appliances, but they refused, continuing their practice of only selling appliances from a manufacturer's catalog. Considering the wage rate in the area averaged twenty-five cents an hour, the

Information on rural electrification was a major attraction at the Taney County Fair, 1950.

merchant's stubbornness was probably sound financial management if not good common sense.

To solve both problems at once, the co-op leaders decided to go into the appliance business. With backing from Noble McCallum, one of the country's largest appliance manufacturers, they put in a small stock of refrigerators, washing machines, hand irons, radios, toasters, and floor lamps at the cooperative office. They obtained a $25,000 loan from the REA and took orders until they had enough to make up a carload. The $25,000 was paid back by the penny-wise farmers, all but $40 that Frank Dawes said, "we lost by giving credit to a 'come-here' from Arkansas that skipped the country in the night." As for the local merchants' reactions to this entrepreneurial success, Frank said, "They were furious over the loss of business; business they might have had if they'd worked with the Co-op."

A Screeching Halt

No sooner did White River get into full swing than the United States entered World War II and, in a startling contradiction, pulled the proverbial plug on rural electrification. At the same time they were asking farmers to increase their productivity to feed the hungry troops, they were denying them the one thing intended to help them do just that—electricity. Apparently, the War Production Board decided copper wire was more critical

Delivering poles for construction of lines in Douglas County, ca. 1950.

for the war effort than for rural power lines. The purchase of wires, poles, transformers, and meters was halted by the government's drive to accumulate enough metal for the war effort. Only projects that were 40 percent or more complete by December 5, 1941, could be finished. Everything else came to a screeching halt.

With their hands tied, the co-op turned away hundreds of people who were coming in to the office requesting service. Frank Dawes recalled being chastised by some who were turned away for not making them sign up earlier. "I had to remind them that we'd used every legal weapon on them but a Billy club and gun."

Poles were raised by hand using pike poles to set them in place.

Norwood Speight was working in the office under Frank Dawes at the time and recalled the compromise the War Production Board struck that allowed farms to be energized provided they had sufficient numbers of livestock. "The government decided that we needed the production on the farms. So they put in a farm unit plan. For instance, if a fellow had six dairy cows, we could build 600 feet to get to him—a hundred feet for each cow. A flock of hens was so many points and that prevailed during the remainder of the war." The result was a domino effect. As Frank Dawes explained, "If the first farm had enough 'units' to allow us to build the line to him and past him far enough for the next farmer to use his units to carry on still further, we were able to keep going." Rumors sprang up that farmers were borrowing their neighbor's livestock on the days the inspector arrived, to the extent the cows became footsore and were unable to graze, lowering milk production to dangerously low levels. Those rumors were never proved nor disproved. Nonetheless, the co-op was able to expand power lines toward Nixa, Sparta, and the Ava area in Douglas County.

The first extension made under the new rules was to the 1,000-acre dairy farm of Myron White, near Highlandville. By the end of 1945 the system had 404 miles of line serving 1,365 members.

In 1946 Frank Dawes resigned as manager of White River Valley Electric Cooperative to become the REA's Chief of Operations Division in Washington, D.C. Norwood Speight stepped into his shoes at White River and with the war over, the co-op faced a backlog created by the materials shortage. "I thought we'd all go crazy," Norwood said, "because there were so many people that had made their application for electricity in Taney, Stone, Christian, Ozark and Douglas Counties that they were calling us night and day and we couldn't get the materials even then after the war. We were so far behind that I don't know how we ever caught up. But we did, and the program kept growing."

With the post-World War II boom looming on the horizon, local merchants agreed to stock appliances and do their part in selling them to the farmers. The co-op happily agreed to exit the appliance business.

In July of 1948, the cooperative installed the first three-phase line in its area from Ava to Gainesville in order to provide three-phase service to the Gainesville Cheese Company. The following year the cooperative installed a two-way radio communication system with

Norwood Speight

Norwood Speight went to work for White River Valley Electric Cooperative on May 28, 1944, and became the co-op's second manager on January 17, 1946. Throughout his career, Speight was a leader in the rural electrification program on the national, regional, state, and local levels though he regarded his assignment as chairman of the Southwest Power Advisory Group as his most rewarding. He was instrumental in procuring the necessary appropriations for Table Rock Dam and other hydro projects. He served on the board of the Association of Missouri Electric Cooperatives (chairing its Legal Services Committee), was vice president of the Sho-Me Power Corporation Board of Directors, and served two years as acting manager of KAMO Electric Cooperative.

Originally a teacher and school administrator, Norwood carried his sense of discipline into the co-op. Recalled Jeri Layton, "He expected people to be there on time and he expected people to work." But his dedication to his family, his church, and his community also came through in his management style. Said Delbert Moore, "You could go in his office and talk to him anytime." When Delbert's wife fell ill, Norwood suggested he take time off to help care for her, assuring him that he could return when he was ready. Norwood Speight retired from WRVEC in January of 1976.

central station units at the Hollister and Ava offices, plus five mobile units. In 1950, 233 miles of new lines were built in Ozark County and another 31 miles of line were enlarged. The White River Valley Electric Cooperative had seventeen employees.

The Survey Shows...

In December of 1949, the *Hill and Holler News* published the results of a survey taken to find out what electrical appliances their members had purchased. Of its 4,000 members, 2,437 responded to the survey. Here's what they learned:

2,162 consumers (89%) had a hand iron;
2,062 or 85% had a radio;
1,760 (72%) had a washing machine;
49% had portable lamps;
38% had a fan;
4% had a toaster and 19% had a vacuum cleaner.

Only 16% of them had running water.

A Boost from Bull Shoals Dam

The demand for power was increasing throughout Missouri and its adjoining states. Congress authorized construction of the Bull Shoals Dam as early as 1941 but like the co-op's lines, it was stalled by World War II. Finally in May of 1947 construction was underway. Although the dam was completed and providing relief from the flooding White River by 1951, the power system installation wasn't slated for completion until 1952.

In the meantime, many of the rural cooperatives went to work lobbying for support for the Southwestern Power Administration (SPA). In May of 1949, Norwood Speight, who was serving as chairman of the Southwest Power Advisory Group, took the train to Washington, D.C., along with many other directors and representatives from over two hundred cooperatives throughout Missouri, Arkansas, Kansas, Oklahoma, Texas, and Louisiana to unite their efforts toward providing the southwest area with adequate, dependable, and low-cost electric power. The consensus among them was that the most efficient and cost-effective way to accomplish this was through the Southwestern Power Administration. "This body," Speight explained, "has asked our federal government for a loan necessary to transmit the electric power from the government dams to the rural cooperatives, city utilities, and other groups needing additional

White River's office was in Hollister from 1945 to 1951.

electric power." The Bureau of the Federal Budget approved Southwestern Power Administration's request.

Congress appropriated another $350 million in loan funds for the REA for fiscal 1950, plus another $150 million if deemed necessary. The June 1949 *Hill and Holler News* reported, "REA's loan policies have been so sound and the repayment record of rural electric cooperatives so excellent that the House feels it can rely on REA and its borrowers to use only that amount of the allocation found necessary. That is about as fine a compliment as can be paid to the program in an era of expanding bureaus and astronomical expenditures."

A portion of that appropriation went to Sho-Me Power Corporation in 1950, when the REA approved their loan request for $2 million. This loan, together with another made to that corporation in March of 1949, made it possible for Sho-Me to construct 371 miles of 69-kilovolt-transmission line. At the time, White River was purchasing power from Sho-Me's 33-kilovolt-transmission line running

Ben Edwards conducts a training class for the White River crews and congratulates them on its completion.

In the early 1950s, employees and members formed the "R.E.A. Circuits" and competed with teams from other co-ops. Back row, L to R: Wayne Goodall, Faye Snowden, Kenton Snowden, and Leroy Freeman. Front, L to R: Cleo Freeman, Dewey Snowden, Clay Cantwell, Jim Wilson, and Coach D. R. Sutherland.

Willie Wiredhand became the familiar mascot for rural electric cooperatives across the country.

Willie Wiredhand

Created by Andrew McLay, an entomologist turned artist who later worked for the NRECA, Willie Wiredhand became the mascot for rural co-ops across the nation on October 30, 1950. His counterpart, Reddy Kilowatt with his lightning bolt body, had been around since 1926. The REA considered adopting Reddy as their own mascot but Reddy's creator Ashton Collins believed that co-ops were "socialistic" and declared that Reddy was reserved for "investor-owned, tax-paying" utilities. Several years after Willie Wiredhand was created, Collins and a group of privately owned utilities filed a federal lawsuit against Willie. After a weeklong trial in January 1956, a U.S. District Court denied Reddy his monopoly. The legal conflict between Willie Wiredhand and Reddy Kilowatt was a symbol for the tension that existed between the co-ops and the commercial power companies.

The phrase, "He's small, but he's wirey," came out of that conflict.

from Mansfield to Ava. That line was rebuilt and made into a 69-kilovolt-transmission line and extended from Ava to Gainesville where White River planned to build a substation.

When President Harry Truman dedicated Bull Shoals Dam on July 2, 1952, he delivered his speech in a white suit and white Panama hat and admonished the private power companies that

Folks crowded into the big tent for the entertainment and news of their co-op at the 1952 annual meeting.

had fought against the dam, pledging to build more in order to get the electricity they produced to the people through the rural electric cooperatives. He announced he'd already asked Congress to appropriate money for Table Rock Dam though it would take several years for work to begin. "Some time or another, we're going to get it done, in spite of all the opposition," he said. Directing his closing comments again to the private power companies, he added, "If it hadn't been for the New Deal and the Fair Deal of the last twenty years, you wouldn't have these dams and these improvements on these other rivers like it. Put that in your pipe and smoke it."

With the new Bull Shoals Dam up and running, Sho-Me Power Corporation completed the planned increase on the lines from Mansfield to Ava and built a new 69-kilovolt-transmission line from Ava to Gainesville. Sho-Me's new substation, located one mile northwest of Gainesville, was energized on November 19, 1952, finally providing an adequate supply of power to Douglas and Ozark counties. At the time, White River was buying almost half of its power from Sho-Me and half from Empire District Electric Company.

About the same time, White River contracted with L P & H Construction Company of Linden, Indiana, for the construction of 136 miles of new electric distribution lines and 12 miles of conversion line for a total of $240,029.76 to get electric service to an additional 232 farms. The co-op's four short-service crews built the one-mile-or-less extensions to another 1,000 farms. Frank Horton & Company of Lamar, Missouri, was awarded the engineering contract putting staking crews to work even before the plans were approved.

The annual meetings began in 1940 and since then, members have gathered annually to enjoy the entertainment, the food, the prizes, and visiting with old friends.

A new truck is admired by all.

White River moved its office from Hollister to Branson in 1951. For a while, window displays encouraged people to purchase new electric appliances.

The Branson Office

The long awaited plan to put a co-op office in Branson edged toward becoming a reality in January of 1950 with the approval of an REA loan that included $72,000 for a new office building. Some years prior, the REA secured land to the north of the Branson Motor Company property where it planned to erect a permanent office. By May of 1951 both the Ava and Gainesville offices had been opened to serve Douglas and Ozark counties giving the co-op one short-service crew, one maintenance crew, and one survey crew at Ava; two crews in Hollister; and combination short-service and maintenance crews at Gainesville and Ozark. Each of these crews had telephone connections and two-way radios to communicate with each other and with the home office at Hollister and the sub-office at Ava, providing the members with a greatly improved response to outages.

The *Hill and Holler News*

When Norwood Speight became manager of White River, one of the things he initiated was a means for communicating regularly with the members. The co-op's newsletter, the *Hill and Holler News*, was mailed monthly to provide members with their directors' names and phone numbers and instructions on what to do in case of an outage or other problem.

It also provided the co-op with an avenue for educating their members on the use of electrical appliances and testimonials from people throughout the area who gave witness to the many ways their lives had been improved and their farms enriched through the use of electrical appliances. It wasn't

Employees gather in the lunchroom in the Branson office.

The White River crew gathers for a group shot outside the Branson office.

Mrs. Polly Hilton

The October 1954 *Hill and Holler News* featured Mrs. Polly Hilton, known as "Ma" to all her friends, then the oldest known member of the co-op and "the oldest Bilyeu living." At age ninety-three, she'd been a widow for forty years and, corncob pipe placed firmly in her mouth, she could still read the *Hill and Holler News* without glasses. She lived at Pine Ridge where she raised eleven children and had left Christian County only twice in her life. She'd only received electricity three years before. "I like the lights fine," she said, "but I'm afraid of electricity."

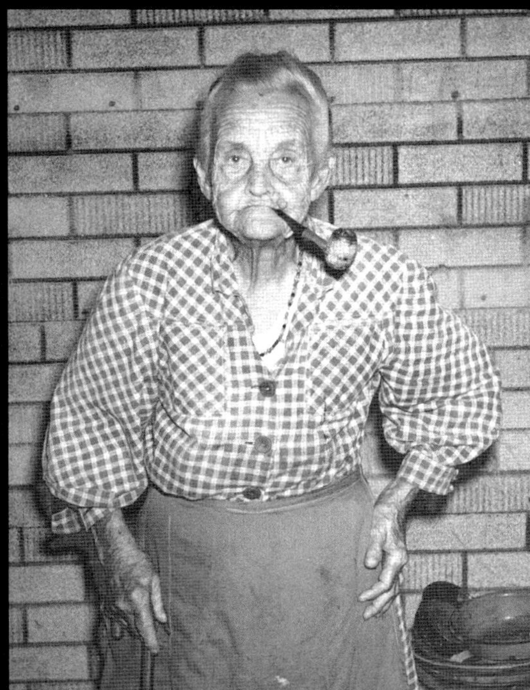

entirely altruistic; the more appliances the members purchased, the more electricity they used and load building was a primary concern for Mr. Speight.

The cover of the May 1951 Hill and Holler *featured a signed Steve Miller drawing for Mother's Day.*

Far from dull, the *Hill and Holler News* was loaded with cartoons, graphics, and the down-home humor for which Branson is still famous. Norwood Speight credited a man named Steve Miller for its creativity and liveliness. "All yours truly had to say to Steve was, 'We want a picture of some woman washing over the old washboard,' and he would come up with the whole thing—a picture and a cover for that magazine," Norwood said. "He'd have the kids barefooted and snotty-nosed with stringy hair, but all you had to do was give him the idea."

To balance the newsletter's business and statistics, Norwood also solicited the writing talents of Mary Elizabeth Mahnkey, a lady he remembered having "lovely white hair and a smile that just radiated all over her face." Mary Elizabeth Prather Mahnkey was born on August 16, 1877, in Harrison, Arkansas, just over the state line from Taney County, Missouri. Her colorful childhood included tales of being run over by a wagon from which she'd been thrown and narrowly escaping Indian captivity until her mother's offer of food and water dissuaded her would-be captors. Her father was a

Having electricity meant different things to different people.

founding member of the Bald Knobbers who eventually helped local law enforcement to shut them down.

For everyone, it meant a better quality of life.

Mary Elizabeth loved to write even as a young girl and eventually earned her teaching degree from normal school. She got her first job at age seventeen in 1894 for which she was paid a salary of $20 a month until she married Pres Mahnkey in 1899. She loved her Ozark home and the people who lived there and wrote about the landscape and its people in a weekly newspaper column for fifty-seven years. In 1943 she was named Poet Laureate of the Ozarks and when Mary Elizabeth died in 1948, her son Douglas filled her shoes writing for the *Hill and Holler News*. With deep roots in the Ozark hills, he loved its history and shared his vast knowledge with the White River members.

The Never Ending Fight

When the REA celebrated its fifteenth birthday on May 11, 1950, they estimated over 80 percent of America's farms had been electrified. Clark T. McWhorton, president of the REA, congratulated the rural co-ops for their success but offered this challenge:

I would offer caution that the never-ending fight is still on—to bring to all the farm people of America the opportunity of sharing fully in the comforts and benefits of modern living and the use of our God-given resources for strength and happiness and security is essential to a strong and mighty America. If we forget or ignore our responsibilities to fight courageously for the principles we believe are right, if we fall prey to blandishments or threats of those who do not believe people have individual rights as great as those of corporations, we will be failing in our responsibilities as citizens, as well as leaders in our own program.

Sources for chapter:
http://www.southshore.com/bsdam.htm#history
www.projecttanny.org/50083/mahnkeyb.html
The Next Greatest Thing, National Rural Electric Cooperative Association, 1984

Chapter Four
Making Progress

People certainly are peculiar—they want the front of the bus, the back of the church, and the middle of the road.

Excerpt from "Grandpa Sez" in the** White River Co-op News**, 1960s

By the middle of 1954, a second year of drought led to the loss of 249 members who were forced to leave their farms and move elsewhere to find employment. In September of that year, the co-op announced plans for a new sub-office at Ava, which opened on April 18 the following year. Located one and a half blocks east of the Ava public square, the building sported the latest technology—a General Electric Weathertron heat pump that cooled the office in summer and heated it during the winter. The lot and building combined cost $24,298.26.

The REA demonstration truck joined the parade for Ozark County's first Dairy Day Festival in Gainesville in June 1955.

Table Rock Dam

Also in 1954, the plans to build the long-awaited Table Rock Dam were announced. Work was set to begin in early October and when completed, the dam was to include a 1,600-foot concrete gravity section in the channel of the White River. Earth embankments of 4,800 feet were planned to join the north and south ends of the concrete section. Ultimately, the dam would rise to 250 feet above the streambed at its highest point and use 1,300,000 cubic yards of concrete. Plans called for four gated penstocks, each 18 feet in diameter, for the operation of four 50,000-kilowatt capacity electric power generators. The contractors

Groundbreaking for Table Rock Dam, 1954.

Ground was broken for Table Rock Dam in 1954 and it was completed in 1959.

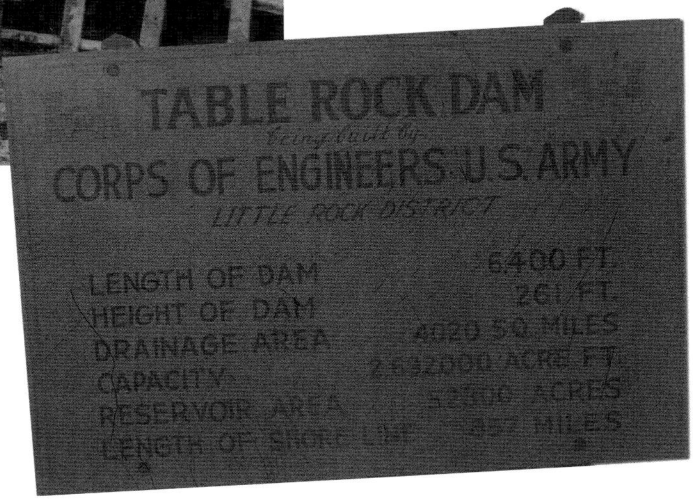

building the dam asked White River Co-op to provide them with 100 kilowatts of electric power at the site to power their equipment and provide floodlights for working at night.

Ironically, during April of 1957, heavy rains and construction on Table Rock Dam caused the White River to flood at Kimberling Crossing. Army engineers and troops from Fort Leonard Wood put a ferry into operation and asked White River Valley Electric Co-op to extend their power line to the north bank of the river so floodlights could be used during the emergency. Two hours and fifteen minutes after receiving the request, two line crews were at the scene, ready to begin construction on the 1,000-foot extension.

The long awaited Table Rock Dam was dedicated on June 14, 1959. A luncheon at the School of the Ozarks preceded the dedication. Norwood Speight, who had long advocated the dam, served as master of ceremonies for the festivities. In his dedication address, Senator Stuart Symington expressed the belief that the beautiful White River region of Missouri would become "the number one recreational area of the Midwest." Following his address, Senator Symington threw the switch in the powerhouse starting the production of electric power.

Wise Power Use Means Savings

The January 1954 edition of the *Hill and Holler News* had some "hard cold facts" about how much time the average farmer could save by using electric appliances. Here are just a few:

> Electric lights in the barn, home, yard and outbuildings can mean another 548 hours a year in chore time.
>
> With an electric iron, washing machine and vacuum cleaner, the average housewife can save 780 hours a year.
>
> An electric light in the henhouse increases egg production 10% or more during fall and winter.

Also included were some tips on using electric lamps for newborn pigs: "In order to supply heat at the most critical period—during the first few hours after birth—one or more 250-watt infrared lamps should be suspended over the farrowing area out of the sow's reach. They should be turned on shortly before the sow is expected to farrow. Within 24 hours after birth the infrared lamps should be moved to a corner brooker, with a barrier to keep the sow from crushing the pigs. Lamp must be used for at least three days to prevent chilling, and a longer period is desired to prevent crushing by the sow."

Upgrading the System

While they awaited the completion of Table Rock Dam, White River was upgrading much of its system, increasing the capacity of its lines throughout the area. The distribution line south of Hollister along Highway 65 to within four miles of the Arkansas state line was converted during June of 1955 making it capable of carrying three times the amount of electricity it previously carried.

In May of 1956, White River received word from Congressman Dewey Short and Senators Symington and Hennings that the REA approved their new loan request for $475,000. "We expect to build eighty-seven miles of new lines to serve 435 new consumers, many of which will be on the shores of the new Table Rock Lake," Norwood Speight reported. "This construction is estimated to cost $261,000."

The June 1957 edition of the *Hill and Holler News* reported a new power source had become available on May 14. The Empire District Electric Company had recently completed a new substation just south of Highway 148, two miles southwest of Reeds Spring. The additional power source made it possible for nine miles of White River's lines to be enlarged and improved for better service to its members. The article added, "The electric lines will be worked 'hot,' so that power interruptions will be kept to a minimum."

Steve Miller, whose comical and heartwarming drawings for years enlivened the Hill and Holler News.

In 1958, Ben Edwards, who was chief engineer for White River, drew up a five-year plan for system improvements that included upgrading 78.25 miles of existing lines at an estimated cost of $96,210. The installation of larger wires and poles enabled the lines to carry the increased power demands being placed on them. "During this same period," Norwood announced, "we expect to improve service by building eighteen miles of tie lines, estimated at a cost of $30,783 and another $136,198.26 will be spent on system improvements and miscellaneous equipment."

"Star of Wonder, Star of Light ......"

See that star atop the tree? Down through the ages, it has been the symbol of wonder and the spiritual light which brings people together—uniting them with the common bond of loving kindness, friendship and cooperation. That same spirit is felt every day of our lives in whatever we do—people working together for the well being of all.

This Christmas, as you look at that star, hundreds of member-consumers along the miles of electric lines—folks like you who know the true meaning of friendship and cooperation—will join you in offering thanks for our many blessings.

From all of us, especially to you, a sincerely warm and happy

Merry Christmas

Copyright, 1955, National Rural Electric Cooperative Association

Willie Wiredhand wishing everyone a Merry Christmas on the December 1955 cover of Hill and Holler News.

First Signs of Growth

Prior to 1959, the co-op's system plans were based on a ten-year projection, but the area was growing in complexity and it was getting more difficult to plan beyond a five-year span. At the time, the co-op's area was approximately 2,400 square miles. Some of it was farmland, some was in rough timber, and the rest ran along the lakes providing a good tourist business. Because the electricity usage varied so much from area to area, the decision was made to divide the area into six-mile-square townships. Averaging the kilowatt-hour usage in each of these smaller township areas made it possible for the co-op to accurately pinpoint the areas where the electric facilities needed to be increased. The goal, of course, was always to assure adequate service at the lowest possible cost to the members.

Engineer Ben Edwards with the White River Board of Directors, early 1950s.

In the meantime, the purpose of the REA was expanded back in 1949 when it received authorization to loan funds for developing telephone service in rural areas. In April of 1959, WRVEC entered into joint-use contracts with area telephone companies to allow telephone lines to be attached to cooperative electric poles. This agreement made it possible for the phone companies to extend telephone service into the rural areas much sooner than it otherwise would have and over the coming years, some 12,000 of White River's poles would be delivering phone service as well as electricity to its members. People gathered in Gainesville on April 16, 1959, to celebrate the start of telephone service for Ozark County. Lt. Governor Edward V. Long made the first call to Congressman Charlie Brown in Washington.

White River employees, among them, seated L to R: Nellie Rea, Margaret Edwards, Peggy Orr, Faye Snowden, Don Baker. Standing L to R: Bob Bennett, Clyde Foley, unknown, Ferris Keith, Charley Miller, Dick Barker, and Lois Kenner. The occasion was the going away party for Don Baker, who was drafted into the military.

Annual Meetings

The August 1959 newsletter reported: "Your directors have signed loan notes with our Federal Government in the amount of $4,923,180. Repayment on principal totals $845,174 as of Dec. 31. We are pleased to report that your co-op has never been late with a payment on principal or interest."

The White River Annual Meeting in Ava, Missouri, June 23, 1953.

It might have been difficult for the rural folks of the Ozarks region to grasp managing large sums of money such as this. If so, their understanding of the co-op's business was assisted through an admirable stream of communication that dated back to the co-op's beginning. In addition to regular editions of the *Hill and Holler News*, the annual meeting provided an opportunity for the members to hear from the co-op's leadership.

The earliest annual meetings were held at the ballpark near Gainesville under a big tent. For many years after that, they were held in Mang Field in Shadow Rock Park at Forsyth. White River employees set up the big tent the night before the meeting, an undertaking that led to a fair amount of horseplay in itself. Set-up began at 7:30 a.m. the day of the meeting to prepare the free coffee and doughnuts. Members sometimes lined up as early as six o'clock that morning. "Free" seems to be a recurring theme for the

At the 1955 annual meeting, electricity was dubbed, "The Farmer's Best Hired Man," and members lined up for free Golden Royal ice cream.

Dudes and Dolls

The entertainment at the 1955 annual meeting included the Dudes and Dolls, a group of youngsters from Forsyth who gave an exhibition of Ozark square dancing; the Ship Ahoys, a group of five women who performed their singing act in Branson; and the Robertson Family. Lonnie, Thelma, and son Jarrett furnished music and songs that included folk, hymns, and instrumentals on the violin and guitar. The Robertson's moved back to their native Ozark County in 1952 and operated Lonnie and Thelma's Court near Lutie, Missouri.

The demonstration truck at the 1956 annual meeting in Branson.

White River Annual Meeting and the frugal Ozark region farmers indulged in the treats that were offered without reservation. Members could be seen consuming copious amounts of soda pop, ice cream, and doughnuts. The year the co-op handed out yardsticks to everyone in attendance, a few members ingeniously used them to create giant doughnut kabobs. For a few years, free lightbulbs helped attract a crowd and every year an astounding list of attendance prizes, donated by local businesses, was awarded. In recent years, the co-op has tried to shift to healthier treats like bottled water and fresh fruit, which seem to be enjoyed just as robustly as ever.

Members came out in droves for White River's annual meeting. Prior to the entertainment boom in Branson, beyond an occasional church supper or family gathering, there weren't a lot of recreational options. Ted Bookout recalled the year the park at Forsyth was covered with water, as it frequently was, and the meeting was moved to the College of the Ozarks. According to Ted, that meeting had the lowest attendance. "People didn't like it because it didn't look like a fair," he explained. Then in 1967 the

The best part of White River's annual meetings is giving long-time friends a chance to catch up on the news and each other.

annual meeting was held under the big top at the Branson ballpark. It might be an indication of how accustomed people have become to air conditioning that they enjoy the current location for the meeting at the Tri-Lakes Center, which locals refer to as the "old Mel Tillis theatre."

Wherever the meeting was held, entertainment was always provided and over the years they've had everything from bluegrass bands to local choral groups to big name entertainers like Roy Clark and Mel Tillis. The biggest name, if not the splashiest act, came to the big tent in 1959 when Paul Harvey was engaged as the guest speaker. The nationally known radio news analyst, newspaper columnist, lecturer, and writer was known for his honesty and straight thinking. That same year, the "Country Gentlemen" of ABC Television's popular *Jubilee U.S.A.* provided the entertainment. Armed with banjos, steel guitars, and base fiddles, Red Foley called them "the best blues-chasin'st act that ever walked out on a stage."

The board of directors welcomes members to the 1956 annual meeting.

Beyond the free ice cream, the lightbulbs, and the entertainment, the most important aspect of the White River Annual Meeting was the opportunity it gave people to come together from the surrounding five counties to make their voices heard. Chris Hamon remembers how much his grandfather,

At the 1959 annual meeting, the "Country Gentlemen" of ABC's popular television show Jubilee U.S.A., *provided the entertainment.*

Robert Hamon, looked forward to the meetings, and how he stood outside the big tent visiting with folks he might have an opportunity to see only once or twice a year. In addition, members voted on their board of directors and learned of the co-op's financial status and its plans for the coming year.

The REA marked its twenty-fourth anniversary on May 11, 1959. Commenting on the co-op's payment record, REA Administrator David Hamil said, "In the latter 1930's, a lot of people were wondering if those new rural electric systems were going to be able to meet the payments on

All eyes were on the stage at the September 1957 annual meeting for the speeches, the entertainment, and the prizes.

There's a Prize for Everything!

Six special prizes were given away at the October 1961 annual meeting:

The prize for being the oldest man went to F. J. Woods of Reeds Spring, age eighty-seven, and the prize for being the oldest woman went to Tolitha Garrison of Sparta, age ninety-one. Both were given an electric heating pad.

Mr. and Mrs. Ed Finney of Chadwick, married sixty-two years, won an electric blanket for being the longest married couple.

The most recently married couple, Mr. and Mrs. Albert Branson of Kirbyville, married just that summer, won an electric fry pan.

The boy under age twelve with the most freckles was Vincent White of Bradleyville and for the girls, Marjorie Pryor of Ozark. Both received a "certified study lamp."

their Government loans when due. Today they have their answer. The rural electrification program has proved one of the soundest investments ever made by the people of this country." As of 1959, REA loans had been used by co-ops and other private organizations to construct 1,480,000 miles of distribution lines to serve 5,140,000 rural consumers.

Paul Harvey autographed Leroy Bowman's copy of the August 1959 Hill and Holler News. *By the mid-1980s, the area's landscape and population had changed dramatically and the* Hill and Holler News *was discontinued. However, White River news appeared regularly, as it does to this day, in* Rural Missouri.

Paul Harvey chums it up with Norwood Speight (left) at the 1959 annual meeting. (Gentleman on the right is unknown.)

Chapter Five
The White River Linemen

"We could never praise enough the fellows that climb the poles and maintain these lines. I just don't think the rural part of America is going to get in too much trouble if they keep the lights on out in the hills and the hollers."

Norwood Speight

Whatever success White River Valley Electric Cooperative has achieved, be it in the modernization of rural farm life, providing customer service, or contributing to the local communities, none of it would have happened without the White River linemen. Like the rural communities they serve, they've seen a great many changes through the years.

L to R: Leonard Sanders, Gilbert Brashears, Waldo Burke, and Foreman Delbert Moore of the Ava short-service construction and maintenance crew which won the distinction (and a chicken dinner) for producing the most work per man hour during 1954.

A Banjo and a Spoon

Carving out a path for the lines through the hills and hollers of the Ozark region was no easy task, and it's hard to say whether those early linemen would be envious or scoff at the equipment today's linemen enjoy. Before digger trucks were available, holes were dug by hand with shovels. With ten-foot long handles, the men called them "a banjo and a spoon" and they filled, dumped, and refilled them until the hole was clean. They were no match for the rocky soil around Branson. For that, you needed dynamite, steady hands, and strong nerves.

1953 Gainesville crew: unknown, Alfred Allen, and Pete Klineline.

L to R: Dan Groves, Tom Stockstill, Foreman Radford McGinnis, and Earnest Jones of the Ozark crew.

Delbert Moore grew up in Ava and got his job with White River just after World War II. He'd been all through Europe as a medic in General Patton's Third Army and he and his brother had both been recently discharged. When someone in the White River office offered Delbert's brother a job, he said yes, but only if they'd take Delbert as well.

He was on a four-year training program to be a lineman and a surveyor. "They put me with two guys in a truck. We dug the holes by hand back then. After a while, if you knew dynamite, you could blow the hole nice and clean." Delbert carried a small box of dynamite and caps in the back of his truck. Without batting an eyelash, he makes something that today's safety regulations would never allow sound like a walk in the park. "You just put that cap in there, put the backer on it, and 'wham,' there it goes!" Once the hole was dug, an A-frame wench was used to put the pole upright and set it in the hole. Digger trucks with their rock-boring augers came on the scene by the mid-1960s.

Most linemen will attest that the biggest change they've seen over the years has been the addition of bucket trucks during the mid-1970s. Delbert Moore had been climbing poles for twenty-five years by the time bucket trucks came along. "I got to where I could scoot up them poles just like a squirrel." Years later, Delbert would

Rubber gloves, safety belt, and gaff hooks—it's not hard to tell which of these men just came down off those substation poles.

With his gaff hooks still strapped to his legs, an early White River lineman points to his work with pride.

become the cooperative's engineer, replacing long-time Chief Engineer Ben Edwards.

Before that, it wasn't uncommon for the linemen to spend eight hours a day on a pole. Carl Hunt remembers many days when he only came down off the pole for lunch. "All of our work on poles we had to do with climbing tools, hooks and belt, and rubber gloves (if we were within four feet of the phase wire), and a hard hat. We carried up a crescent wrench, a screwdriver, pliers, hammer and a wooden ruler because when you go up there you've got to measure everything. We carried a hand line—a rope with a pulley on it so the guy on the ground could send up whatever you needed."

Essential to the linemen were good boots with a strong arch support and a set of sharp gaff hooks that strapped on under the knee and at the ankle.

Training

When White River started out, all training was on-the-job and, despite the hazards, men were eager for the work and opportunity. New hires started, quite literally, at the ground level, working for two years as a groundsman feeding materials up to the lineman on the pole. Roy Grady worked for White River for forty years and when he was hired, groundsmen served an eight-year apprenticeship to become journeymen. "We just jumped in," he recalled. "Some of the training was rough, but you didn't forget it."

The first practical technical schooling came along in 1979 and most linemen attended the three-year training at night classes. The groundsman classification has since been eliminated and new hires now start as apprentice linemen. Their training begins on the job with additional classroom work, and they serve a four-year apprenticeship before becoming a journeyman lineman. The benefit is that, when a storm hits and creates widespread outages, there are more men to call on to help get through the crisis.

The Extendo

November 1971

Before Nintendo, there was the Extendo, a telescoping hotstick that made it possible for the linemen to energize transformers or change transformer fuses from the ground, saving dangerous and time-consuming pole climbing. Only five feet long when collapsed, the fiberglass stick extended to over forty feet in length.

On-the-job training changed farmers into White River linemen.

Right-of-way clearing crew in the 1950s. Left to right: Frank Howard, A. Buck, Frank Davis, and Howard Bryant.

White River linemen in front of the Branson office, ca. 1958.

Front, L to R: Bill Collins, Carl Hunt, Clyde Foley, and Pete Klineline. Back, L to R: Earl Petro, Harrison Allen, and Quentin Johnson, 1963.

White River line crew, 1966. Front row, L to R: Elmer Johnson, Carl Hunt, Troy Beal, Wayne McFarland, Clarence Thurman, Bill Collins, Pete Klineline, Delbert Moore, Radford McGinnis, Ernest Jones, Bob Large, Chuck Rees. Back row, L to R: Ernie Thurman, Quentin Johnson, Paul Scowden, Russell Klineline, Jim Bane, John Chaney, Harrison Allen, Austin Brittain, Leonard Sanders, Lyle Ray, Earl Petro, George Robests, Clyde Foley.

A Tribute to Norman (Bing) Gardner

The August 15, 1947, edition of the *White River Leader* reported the death of Norman (Bing) Gardner. At age thirty-two, Mr. Gardner was killed on August 9 while running a third wire for Mr. and Mrs. Ed King, long-time co-op members. An employee of the WRVEC since 1941, Mr. Gardner was a construction foreman and was belted to a line pole to which were attached two 110-volt wires below a high line. Though the article said they were uncertain how the accident happened, veteran linemen explained the line had been turned on before he completed the wiring, a hazard in the days before radio communication. Mr. Gardner was born in Taney County in 1915, and the article described him "as a kind man who could be relied on for even the toughest of jobs."

In the days before safety gear, linemen donned everyday clothes to work.

Setting poles, 1953

The Branson crew in 1953. Left to right: Paul Scowden, Bob Large, Ernest Thruman, and O. H. Gentry.

Carl Hunt, Gainesville foreman, energizing a new transformer (left), 1970.

Safety

Despite all the changes in training and equipment, the most important change the White River linemen have seen is in safety. Gary Soutee, a White River lineman for thirty-eight years, recalled, "Thirty years ago, you'd kill a line, and you'd just go up and start working—we wouldn't even ground the line. I think we were supposed to, but the awareness wasn't there or something. Now you go through all the steps to make sure it's safe. We ground everything."

Even from the beginning, hard hats and rubber gloves that insulated the linemen should they accidentally touch a hot wire were essential. Said Roy Grady, "You had to wear gloves if you were on the pole. They probably kept me alive a time or two." Now, they have fire retardant shirts and jeans for extra protection.

Working on the lines is and always has been a hazardous job. Even in the late 1950s, line upgrades were occasionally done between midnight and 4 a.m. with the lines hot to minimize interruption in service. Nowadays, the high amperage on the lines poses an even greater danger.

Interviewer: "What was your best day on the job?"

Bill Davis: "I don't remember that day."

Late in 1973 the co-op purchased two new one-man bucket trucks to be based at Branson and Ava, a two-man bucket truck, and an additional digger truck. With these hydraulic powered units, over time much of the climbing of poles

Thank You!

An ice storm in December of 1972 caused the downing of Sho-Me's line cutting off power to Ava and many members served by White River Electric. While other people lost power for as long as nine days, White River Electric members lost power for only a few hours. White River sent help to a neighboring co-op to the northwest, Ozark Electric Co-op at Mount Vernon. One two-man crew worked three days and another worked two days in the Mount Vernon area.

The February 1973 *Co-op News* paid tribute to the linemen: "When the weather goes on a rampage, as it did recently, he must leave his home, go out and engage in a personal battle with the elements of nature. Stormy weather increases the hazards of his job. The lineman seems to be endowed with a special brand of fortitude, endurance, patience and perseverance. Although these men are trained in safe working habits, their job can be very hazardous during storms and especially at night. The electric linemen deserve our thanks and gratitude—and patience—when storms knock out our electric service."

Linemen work to change out a pole using a "hot stick," which allowed the line to stay energized.

was eliminated and the fiberglass bucket insulated on a fiberglass boom made working on three-phase electric lines, which often had to be worked "hot," much safer. The additional digger truck virtually eliminated the once tedious job of hand digging and blasting holes for poles.

No matter how many safety precautions are taken, accidents still happen and there's no telling where the next hazard will come. For instance, Bill Davis remembered the time he was sending a line up to the guy on the pole when two horses running across the field caught the line. In the blink of an eye it wrapped around his hand and pulled him twenty-five feet off the ground.

Kenny Bilyeu has been off the job only three days in twenty-five years because of one incident. "We were stringing a new line across the highway and we forgot to leave anybody on the highway (to divert traffic). A trash truck came down the highway, caught the wire and I got hung up on it at the other end of the job. It dragged me for a ways before it let me go." The jolt dislocated his shoulder, knocked him unconscious, and creased his hard hat. "If it hadn't been for my hard hat, it would have killed me," he said, adding, "When they got to me, they thought it was really bad because I was bleeding out of my ear." Fortunately, the bleeding was from a relatively minor cut.

Storms, particularly ice storms like this one in February of 1973, are the bane of the lineman's existence.

Storms and Other Outages

The one thing the White River linemen are most united on is their dislike of storms. Whether there's a driving wind, freezing ice, pelting rain, or lightning, they all pose hazards. "You can count on being out during the worst of the weather," Bill Davis said. "Ice, cold, lightning—even extreme heat will cause problems. As a lineman, when the weather is at its worst, you're gonna' be there."

"You hate to see them happen," Chris Hamon observed, "but the storms have a way of bringing the crews together." Delbert Moore recalled their crews working three days straight to get lines back up after a tornado at Rockaway Beach in 1975. Downed trees prevented them from getting their trucks in. "We ran out of crews," he said, "but that's just how it was. If there was a storm or something, you'd just as soon get ready to go." That hasn't changed. When the ice storm hit in January of 2009, Chris Hamon proudly remarked, "Our linemen fought the freezing temperatures and dangerous conditions for six days vowing not to stop until power had been restored to every member."

Right-of-way clearing has done more than anything to improve their safety and their working conditions by minimizing power outages due to storms. Still, as Bill Davis said, "The worst is the ice storms. You're

It wasn't uncommon for linemen to spend eight hours straight on a pole, coming down only for lunch.

out in the woods and limbs and sometimes whole trees are still falling. You hear that crack and you just don't know if it's gonna' get you." For Carl Hunt, windstorms were the worst. Side winds can push a lineman's gaff hooks right out of the pole causing him to slide down burning his arms, and he recalls getting "splinters as big as pencils."

It isn't always storms that cause the outages, however. Animals get into substations to escape the cold or hunt prey and the linemen have pulled their fair share of fried snakes and squirrels out of the lines. Carl Hunt once brought such a squirrel back to the office to show the girls and caused quite a commotion when the squirrel, badly stunned but not dead, came back to life on one of their desks.

In the mid-1960s, digger trucks made life a lot easier for the linemen. Bottom photo, they're digging at the KOA campground in Branson, 1984.

It's All In Fun

When the daily job has this many risks, humor usually slips into the equation in order to break the tension, and the linemen of White River are no exception. For instance, Roy Grady told of the time "someone" brought a hornet's nest they'd found into the office. When the hornets warmed up, they came swarming out of the nest. "Norwood like to fired whoever it was that brought it in," Roy said. "As it turned out," he said with a sly grin, "nobody had been working that day. John (Chaney) didn't deny it, I didn't deny it…we just said nothing."

Carl Hunt told the story of the time he'd told a member he'd send a lineman out to assemble a meter loop they'd purchased, an unpopular task. "The lineman went down and finished the job for them and then came back for lunch," Carl said. "While we were eating, the guy said, 'If I knew who told them we would put that meter loop together I'd throw him in the creek!' I threw my sandwich down on the table, got up and told him, 'Let's go.' We went to the creek and both ended up getting wet. Even the girls in the office followed us down to the creek. Nobody was mad—it was all fun."

John Chaney energizing the Gretna substation, June 1979.

Rookies often came under fire, like the time Bill Davis was given the task of putting up a string of dollies on three poles—something he'd never done before. Figuring he'd have to climb each pole separately his crewmates all said, "No, no! Go across the wire—the strut guy." "So I got up there," Bill recalled. "I started out head first and I was doing good until I got to the other pole and the only part of me I could get to the pole was my head. There was nothing to do but go back and by that time they were rolling with laughter." The next time, Bill started feet first.

Turnabout is fair play, however, and once when John Chaney, a bear of a man, used his size thirteen shoes to kick Bill's feet right out of the pole, Bill got him back by nailing his belt to the pole and taking the hammer back down with him. And there was the time that a young Chris Hamon engaged in a silicone war with one of the linemen from Ava. Silicone was used to seal the hole up when laying underground wires and it occasionally showed up inside boots, gloves, or on car door handles. "I loaded up his car with silicone not knowing it was his wife's car. The next day she was going down the road and it was raining so when she turned the windshield wipers on, it coated the whole windshield."

White River Members

White River's first linemen grew up in the area, fishing and hunting throughout it and knew every creek and curve. Directions to outages were often as simple as, "Down by the old Grady place, behind the red barn." As Chris Hamon said, "If they hired someone from outside the area, they had a really big learning curve." These days, modern GPS systems have made locating service calls much

Bucket trucks were a knee-saver for linemen when they came on the scene in the mid-1970s. Here they're working on Highway 65 south of Hollister in 1981.

Lonnie Kaneaster and Delbert Moore at the co-op's first aid training, 1981.

more efficient. But beyond the simple geography, the relationship between the linemen and the members was different in those early years. "In those days," Chris explained, "the linemen knew the members and the members knew them," creating instant trust. Delbert Moore recalled the days when they were first installing lines. "People fed the crew their noonday meal—almost anything they wanted. Hospitality was important to country people."

In the early years, electricity was a luxury and people might go days before reporting an outage or ask that a repair be done "when it's convenient." Even years later, people understood the power had to be turned off for the installation of lines and as long as it was back on in time for the evening milking, everyone was happy. "Now," Chris observed, "it's about data transfer. Electricity is about making the information age work."

Delbert Moore and Chris Hamon working on SCADA, 1988.

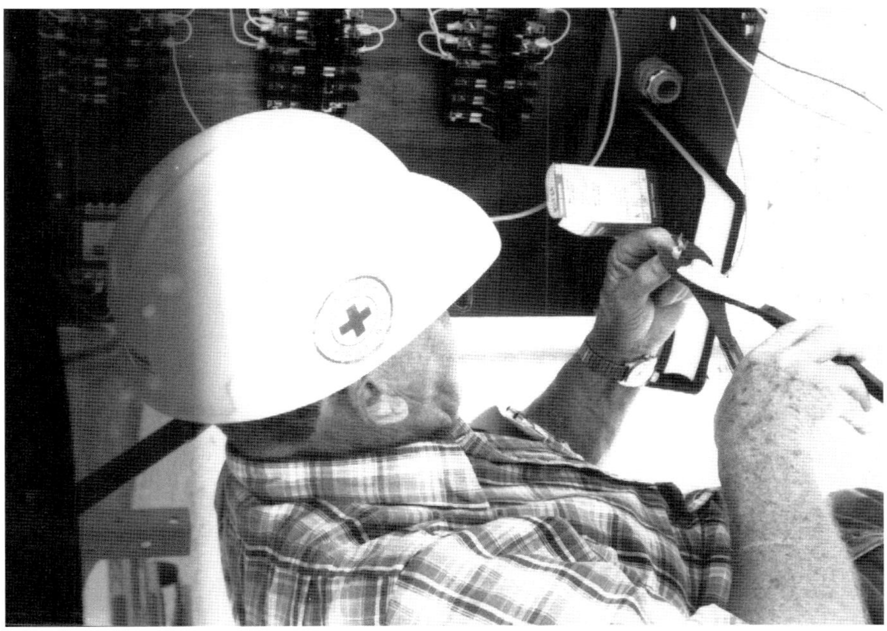

The annual meeting "fun" started early for the linemen whose job it was to put up the tents.

Accessing poles is another problem as people become increasingly protective of their property. "We worked with people for years and if you had the truck out in their field, it was no big deal... they never said nothing," Bill Davis commented. Nowadays the linemen sometimes have to employ diplomacy to access a line and occasionally smooth things over, literally and figuratively. On one occasion Roy Grady barely missed being fired when a Chicago transplant to the area was overly vocal in his suggestions that they do things Chicago-style. "I just looked up at him and said, 'Then, what are you doing in Cedar Creek?' He took it to the big boss."

Sometimes, however, the area's diversity lends some humor to the situation. One time, Gary Soutee, John Chaney, and Lonnie Kaneaster went out on a trouble call to a nearby mall. One of the stores was owned by an Asian couple who spoke limited English. They changed out the transformer and just as Lonnie was calling in to have the line turned on, the lady walked over to John and asked when the power would be on. As Gary Soutee told it, "John looked at her smiling and said, 'Let there be light!' and Bam, it was on! She looked at him and said, 'How you do that?' It couldn't have been timed any more perfectly."

Of all the challenges the linemen face, the one they dread the most is dealing with accounts that are delinquent

Long-time linemen Pete Klineline, Bill Davis, and Lyle Ray, early 1980s.

enough to merit having the power shut off. While an occasional tongue-lashing isn't uncommon, Carl Hunt once found himself threatened with a shotgun. "The guy said to me, 'If you take my meter out, I'm gonna' get my gun out and shoot you.' I said, 'Have you got anything against me?' He said, 'Well, no. I just don't want you to take my meter out.' I said, 'All right, then. I'll have the other guy do it.' His wife came out then and asked what all the fuss was about and when I told her she said, 'I'll be in to pay it Monday.' I said, 'Okay' and they were never delinquent after that."

Yesteryear's linemen faced the difficulty of working at the top of a pole for hours at a time and today's linemen face the backbreaking job working on underground lines. Years ago, the linemen were lucky to have two weeks out of the entire year that they weren't on call. Even now, there are seven people on call, twenty-four hours a day, seven days a week to serve more than 50,000 metered accounts. Today's White River linemen keep 5,412 miles of line up and running. Carl Hunt probably summed up their sentiments the best when he said, "I wouldn't take anything for my experiences at White River—from working in the office, to digging the holes, to collecting bills. I'll just put that last on the list."

Standing on trailer: Kenny Martin, Keith Essick. Standing from left: Mike Jones, Jeff Wasson, Gragg Alms, Rusty Sanders, Larry Maric, Troy Shrope, Joe Wilson, and Blaine Scobee.

Chapter Six
The Good Old Days Come to a Close

"One of the first things Norwood Speight taught us was to never say, 'I don't know.'"

Alta Mae Cary

Everything changes; everything evolves. In the coming decades, the White River Valley Electric Cooperative would have to adjust to massive changes in the communities it served and a changing national energy landscape.

When the Hugo Herschend family, visiting from Chicago, developed Marvel Cave and Silver Dollar City in 1960, they threw the door to Branson wide open. About the same time, Table Rock Dam created Table

1960 annual meeting in Branson.

Rock Lake with its 745 miles of shoreline ripe for restaurants, resort hotels, marinas, and private residences. The White River Valley was no longer a strictly agricultural area as tourism began competing for the top slot. Kimberling City itself was formed solely as a result of Table Rock Lake and in 1966, the old road that ran along the ridge tops from Springfield to Branson was replaced by the new Highway 65, making it much easier for visitors to reach the lakes.

Norwood Speight gives an update on the co-op's finances and "The Waymakers" of Chestnut Ridge provided the entertainment at the September 10, 1960, annual meeting.

In January of 1960 White River opened a sub-office in Gainesville and obtained a loan from the REA for $1,034,000. More than half the funds were to be used to build 150 miles of new distribution lines to 900 new consumers, the majority of which were located on or near the banks of Lakes Table Rock, Taneycomo, and Bull Shoals. By the end of 1960, the cooperative had 2,594 miles of distribution line serving 7,809 consumers. The average monthly consumption of electricity, especially in the Tri-Lakes area, was doubling approximately every seven years.

All the necessary factors existed for affordable energy: increased population, increased demand, and a dependable supply of wholesale electric power. In November of 1963, the board voted to reduce rates to their members, reducing the minimum bill from $2.25 per month to $1.80 per month for 29 kilowatt-hours. According to manager Norwood Speight, "The lower rate is intended as an incentive to make greater use of electricity, thereby improving our members' living standards." In 1965, the U.S. Department of Agriculture announced that 188 rural electric systems across the country currently financed by the REA, White River among them, were able to cut their retail power rates to consumers during 1965. Secretary of Agriculture Orville L. Freeman called the rate reductions "a magnificent response

A Tragic Dispute

A bizarre and tragic episode of public relations gone awry took place one night in 1960 when a man named Bill Jenkins of Taneyville, frustrated with how long it was taking to get electricity to his farm, knocked at the Speight family's front door just as they were sitting down to dinner. Mark Speight, Norwood's son, was in seventh grade at the time and was looking forward to an evening spent with his dad at a scout meeting. Mark answered the door and then went to fetch his father. The family went on with dinner and after a few moments, Mark went back to see what was happening and, to the young boy's horror, discovered his father was gone.

Mr. Jenkins took Norwood at gunpoint back to his farm and made him cut down trees to show him what he had to do without electricity. Satisfied that he'd made his point, Jenkins told Norwood, "Leave the axe here and I'll take you home. I don't think I'll need to hold a gun on you back to Branson. I'm a pretty big man."

Safely back at his home, Norwood called the county sheriff and reported the incident. According to the newspaper account, Sheriff Roy Wade, Deputy Theron Gideon, and Lieutenant Wickham of the Missouri Highway Patrol went to Jenkins's home. Jenkins shot and injured Sheriff Wade but was not apprehended.

The next day Deputy Gideon and other officers returned to the home. Tear gas shells were fired into the house, gunfire ensued, and when the officers used an armored car to batten a hole in the house, they looked in to find Jenkins's body on the floor.

The event even made the network news. "Paul Harvey had been at the White River Annual Meeting just a year or so before and recognized my father's name," Mark recalled. "When it came across the wire, he put it on the news."

to President Johnson's plea to Americans to hold the price line to prevent inflation."

Leroy Bowman, Power Use Adviser, prepared and broadcast messages over local radio stations and did heat-loss calculations for members. His articles in the *Hill and Holler News* covered proper wiring techniques, appliance safety, and often featured farmers and homemakers proudly displaying ways that electricity was now providing them with more ease and greater efficiency and production.

In March of 1960 Ted Bookout joined the co-op as Leroy Bowman's assistant. Ted assisted members in the proper design of electric heating and lighting systems and visited hundreds of members' homes, interviewing them and taking photographs for feature stories in the *Hill and Holler News.*

As members acquired new electric appliances their bills also increased, and when an angry member came into the office, it was often Alta Mae Cary's job to smooth things over. "One of the first things Norwood Speight taught us," she said, "was never to say, 'I don't know.' Instead, we learned to say, 'I'm not too sure about that but I'll find out.'" Her remedy for inaccurate meter readings was simple: "I trained people to take a pencil outside to the meter and write the numbers down so they didn't forget and transpose the numbers."

Gurley Seay, co-op meter inspector and supervisor, uses his TESCO test board at the Branson office where he checked some of the 2,500 meters he tested every year.

Nonetheless, the days of "use more, pay less" were about to come to an end. The increase in demand meant large sums of money for capital investment. In 1967, White River constructed 27.5 miles of line to serve 340 new members and converted many miles of existing line to three-phase service. In August of 1971, KAMO Electric Cooperative began operating a new 5,000-kilovolt-amp substation to supply electricity to White River's lines. The new Kimberling City substation was the tenth KAMO built to serve White River due to growing demand in the area.

The 1964 annual meeting.

The continued growth in the region led to better roads and when State Highway 160 at Gainesville was being surveyed for straightening and improvements, it soon became apparent the White River sub-office and warehouse would be almost in the middle of the new road. The highway department purchased the building and the office was moved temporarily to an old

Frank Dawes, pictured here in 1965 with Georgia Young and Eunice Beasley judging the essay-writing contest, was the first president of White River's Board of Directors and the first manager.

Willie Wiredhand made an appearance at the 1966 annual meeting.

theatre building near the Gainesville post office. Construction then began on a new 4,000 square-foot office and warehouse just south of the old location on the bank of Lick Creek. The new building was occupied May 13, 1974. Compared to the previous 750 square-foot building, the new Gainesville office had a drive-up window, a covered front entry, a conference room, and private offices. The garage had room for storing five trucks and included a 63-foot loading dock.

That same year saw the completion of the new Branson office as well. Opened in October of 1974, the new building boasted 13,500 square feet of office space and 5,400 square feet of garage and storage space. It, too, had a drive-up window and a meeting room with seating capacity for one hundred people with an adjoining kitchen, which was made available to local non-profit organizations.

When the co-op moved from Hollister to its first office in Branson in July of 1951, they were serving 5,270 consumers from 1,847 miles of line. Twenty-three years later the co-op was serving 14,433 consumers over 3,089 miles of line. At the dedication of the new Branson office, Norwood Speight reflected that, in that time period, the average member's usage had increased from 120 kilowatt-hours per month to 1,109 kilowatt-hours per month. "Our cooperative is thirty-five years old," he said. "Many

Sometimes Ted Bookout had to come up with inventive ways to make a point, even for the simplest of issues. He set up an eye-catching True-False Quiz Panel at the Douglas County Fair in October of 1966, giving fairgoers a chance to win a 100-watt Eye Saver lightbulb. To help people understand the difference between the financing entity and their local cooperative, one of the True-False questions was, "REA and White River Electric Co-op mean the same."

of our members today helped organize the cooperatives. Today we serve a new generation of member-consumers, many of whom have never lived in a home without electric lights and running water, refrigeration and central heating."

Political Resistance

The administration of Richard Nixon proved unfriendly to the REA and its co-ops. When Congress failed to make enough loan funds available to the REA to meet the growing demand in 1969, the co-ops were forced to form the National Rural Utilities Cooperative Finance Corporation, more commonly referred to as the CFC.

Then, on December 29, 1972, a day the REA would dub "Black Friday," the Nixon administration announced the termination of the REA loan

By 1968, Branson was a bustling tourist town and signs strung across the busy street welcomed co-op members to the annual meeting.

Comparison of costs, 1944 to 1974

	1944	1974
100 kilowatt-hours	$5.65	$5.60
200 kilowatt-hours	$8.15	$7.60
500 kilowatt-hours	$15.65	$12.70
1,000 kilowatt-hours	$28.15	$21.20
35-foot pole	$18.34	$99.82
40-foot pole	$23.66	$130.09
E1-2 Guy:	$2.13	$16.36
1,000-foot wire:	$18.38	$69.78

At one time, people feared electricity was unsafe. By the 1970s children were often featured in the Hill and Holler News *enjoying its benefits.*

program. The Department of Agriculture issued a press release saying future loans would no longer be made under the Rural Electrification Act but instead under a new Rural Development Act, HB 12931 signed into law on August 30, 1972. President Nixon called for revisions to the REA loan process, among them a reduction in the subsidy inherent in the 2 percent loans.

Rallying a grass roots effort of protest, 1,400 representatives from rural electric cooperatives flocked to Washington in late January 1973 to protest Nixon's action. They returned again in May to urge Congress to pass new legislation restoring the REA, which it did by an overwhelming margin. President Nixon signed the bill that expanded financial resources available to both rural electric and telephone cooperatives into law on May 11, 1973, the thirty-eighth anniversary of the REA.

By the mid-1970s, the region was seeing more than just increased tourist traffic; people were moving to the area in droves in search of the recreational lifestyle. They no longer wanted to visit the area—they wanted to live there. The Tri-Lakes area of Table Rock, Taneycomo, and Bull Shoals saw a tremendous boom in commercial growth. During 1977, 1,007 new members were provided with service, 67 miles of line were built, and new plant investments totaled $1,281,642. The challenge then for the White River Valley Electric Cooperative was to meet the financial obligations of building miles of line between points of existing service.

Superintendent Clyde Foley and Chief Engineer Ben Edwards review plans at the Gainesville substation.

As the population increased, it became necessary to provide three-phase service at an even greater cost.

HB 1092

It was inevitable the increased commercial and residential business that came with the area's growth would catch the attention of the private power companies who had originally shunned the rural business opportunity. As a result, new lines began springing up, built over and around existing lines at greater expense and danger than the original lines.

The REA's rules required the rural cooperatives serve everyone in their area who requested service but were excluded from towns whose population exceeded 2,500 except for members who were annexed into a city. Yet the private power companies had no such restrictions and were free to leapfrog existing lines to pick up profitable accounts.

Energizing the Kimberling City substation, 1971.

During the 1970s, WRVEC had its hands full keeping up with the growth in Branson and surrounding areas.

In 1972, Missouri's rural electric cooperatives banded together, taking their grievances to the Public Service Commission. Norwood Speight and other co-op representatives served on a special legislative committee meeting with state legislators. HB 1092 was introduced which was intended to assign territories for all power suppliers to guard against the unsightly and hazardous duplication of lines.

The private power companies argued before the Public Service Commission that it was, in fact, the rural cooperatives that were encroaching on their territory. Powerless to do anything, the PSC's only response was it would take a legislative act to resolve the dilemma and, ultimately, passage of the bill was never secured.

Several years later, General Manager Larry Frazier served on a statewide committee to address the issue. The duplicated lines, particularly in Branson, made it possible for disgruntled customers to simply switch their service from one company to another, leaving the power providers to bear the cost of switching out meters. The legislation the committee ultimately proposed was signed by Governor Joe Teasdale, and while it didn't provide territorial protection, it ended the practice of switching providers.

Operation Peak Alert

Unlike the early years when peak usage meant the evening milking of cows, peak usage now meant a significantly increased population arriving home from work or school and simultaneously turning on televisions, radios, washing machines, dryers, and stoves. As air-conditioned homes became common, the capacity needed to handle the summer load resulted in excess capacity the rest of the year and for a few years the cooperative offered a lower winter rate. By 1974, winter usage increased to match the summer load and with wholesale power costs rising due to coal costs, the winter rate was discontinued.

On January 1, 1976, Larry Frazier became general manager of the co-op upon Norwood Speight's retirement after almost thirty years as general manager. Later that year, the Association of Missouri

Electric Cooperatives launched a statewide program called Operation Peak Alert to ensure the most efficient and economical use of existing generation and transmission equipment. Members were urged to curtail usage during emergencies to avoid the high cost of purchasing supplemental power.

Operation Peak Alert was first tested as a result of record cold temperatures on New Year's Eve, 1976. Associated Electric Cooperative, Inc., in Springfield, which monitored the statewide REC system, saw the electrical demand rapidly increasing the afternoon of December 30. When it became apparent the peak was going even higher on December 31, Operation Peak Alert was put into effect; pre-arranged TV and radio announcements were broadcast asking REC members to stagger or delay the use of some of their

Beaver Creek Park at Kissee Mills was inundated by floodwaters during the spring of 1973. With the fairgrounds flooded at Shadow Rock Park in Forsyth, that year's annual meeting was moved to College of the Ozarks (below).

Larry Frazier

Larry Frazier graduated from high school in West Plains, earned his degree in business at Southwest Missouri State, and did his postgraduate work at Washington University in St. Louis. He served four years in the army where he received the United States Commendation Medal. Before joining White River, he was president of the Rhodes Supply Company in Springfield.

As general manager of White River, Larry will admit to having a reputation for being "tight," having made it his goal to increase the net worth of the co-op, a goal he achieved with the support of an "excellent board of directors." On the subject of farmer directors, he is surprisingly passionate, saying, "When I hear someone question a farmer being a director, all I can think is, 'I'll bet you couldn't make a living farming.'" He added, "Some of the directors had reservations about me since I came from the Springfield area, but I told them I was born in Christian County and convinced them I was just as big a hillbilly as they were."

Asked to reflect on his White River years he emphasized two things: "I did my job and I started Operation Round Up," a concept he borrowed from a manager/friend at the Hilton Head, North Carolina Co-op. Though he faced some initial opposition, Larry insisted 20 percent of the funds go to scholarships for local students. "I grew up poor. I know what a difference an education can make."

electric appliances. In just a few hours, the demand began leveling and then dropping as 356,000 rural electric cooperative members voluntarily reduced their demand by an estimated 50,000 kilowatts.

The records show that White River's members were indeed conserving energy. The sales of electricity on co-op lines during 1975 were 14.8 percent higher than in 1974 but from 1975 to 1976 they only increased by 6.9 percent. Articles in the *Hill and Holler News* continued to promote the use of adequate insulation, storm doors and windows on older homes and new construction, the correct use of fireplaces and water heaters, and adjusted thermostat settings.

Welding class graduation in the mid-1970s.

Larry Frazier, Glenn Harnden, State Representative Emery Melton, and Roy Matthews at a board meeting, 1979.

Ben Edwards started work as an engineer for White River on April 16, 1946. He was made chief engineer and assistant manager three years later. At his retirement party in March of 1976, Ben said his greatest satisfaction was helping to bring electricity to those who had never known its benefits.

Oliver Gentry

Oliver Gentry was born in 1924 and lived all his life in Ava, Missouri. His parents farmed and the crops and cattle they raised kept them fed through the Great Depression. His father died when Oliver was just twelve years old and when he went into the United States Navy in 1944, his mother sold off the farm; some of it to Oliver's siblings. Though he was stateside for most of his tour of duty, Oliver ended up on Okinawa as part of the amphibious force. From there he went on to China "to help put the Marines on the beach so they could help the Chinese corral the Japanese."

After the war, Oliver went to work for White River Valley Electric Cooperative in August of 1946, starting out as a chainman on the survey crew. His training was on-the-job and when the transit man left, Oliver took over his job in 1948—taking over the entire crew in 1951. Cliff Robertson managed the Ava office at the time so Oliver found himself working for someone he'd known all his life. He also married Allie Miller, a young lady he met at the skating rink in Ava, now his wife of sixty-three years.

His crew worked in all five counties and Oliver describes Ben Edwards as "the best boss I ever had." When folks saw the staking crew come through, they assumed they'd be getting electricity in a few days. "You had to explain that there was a lot of work to be done yet to get them electricity," he said.

Oliver remembers all too well the days without electricity and the sense of mission they had in bringing it to the White River Valley region. "I really think we brought a lot of pride to Missouri," he said. "I'm glad I had something to do with it. About a year and a half after I started, I was surveying the land where I was born and raised. It had been quite a while since I'd lived there, but I was getting it for them." Oliver retired in 1989.

Despite their best efforts at containing costs White River was forced to announce increased rates in February of 1977. White River's wholesale electricity cost was 34.68 percent higher in 1976 than in 1975 and they were now facing another 25 percent increase from its two power suppliers.

When the increased rates were announced, Manager Larry Frazier reassured members that a power cost adjustment would not be applied unless the cost of wholesale power exceeded 20.5 mills per kilowatt-hour. By April, however, the co-op was facing wholesale costs of 26.02 per kilowatt-hour.

Because power suppliers had to have generating capacity adequate to meet peak demand, a "ratchet clause" allowed them to pass the costs they incurred in providing additional power to the distributing cooperative, which then imposed a power cost adjustment to the members. The resulting demand charge then remained, over and above what was actually used, until a higher peak demand was established. Extremely cold weather in January of 1977 sent White River to an all-time high peak demand of 54,898 kilowatt-hours. The members of White River were again called on to be mindful to stagger their energy usage during peak periods.

Complicating things even further, the United Mine Workers of America launched a national coal strike in December of 1977, forcing Missouri rural electric cooperatives to purchase higher cost power generated by oil and gas plants in states in the South and West. General Manager Larry Frazier urged members to decrease their use of this more expensive power from the oil and gas fired plants. Fortunately, the strike ended in March of 1978 and though the additional cost for each cooperative member amounted to 1.5 cents per kilowatt-hour, an average of $15 per month per member, rural electric cooperative officials across the state opted to delay passing on the increased cost to their members. Said Frazier, "Local co-op members were asked early in the coal strike to conserve electricity in order to stretch out the coal supplies on hand and help hold down our purchase of the more expensive power."

Leroy Bowman performing an energy audit for a member in 1981 and top, just before his retirement in 1984.

Sources for chapter:
http://www.rurdev.usda.gov/rbs/pub/may10/out.htm
Keck, Richard P., *Reevaluating the Rural Electrification Administration: A New Deal for the Taxpayers, Environmental Law,* 16 ENTL. L. 39 (1985)
The Next Greatest Thing, National Rural Electric Cooperative Association, 1984.

Chapter Seven
Going High Tech

"As the walls of the old building go down and the walls of the new building go up, the one thing that stays consistent is the heart of the membership."

Chris Hamon

Growth once again provided a major challenge for the people of White River Valley Electric Co-op in the 1980s and into the 1990s. The fastest growth occurred in Christian County; commercial growth was greatest in Kimberling City and Branson where the hotels, resorts, and shopping centers required larger loads. Even Ozark and Douglas counties, which remained largely rural, experienced steady growth.

Because of inflation and environmental issues surrounding Missouri's high sulfur coal, Associated Electric Cooperative, who owned the mines, was forced to exit the coal business in Missouri and start using western coal from Wyoming to generate power in order to comply with the Clean Air Act of 1970. Once they did, the co-op's costs dropped dramatically, western coal being much cheaper than Missouri's high sulfur coal.

A crowd of more than two thousand attended the forty-first annual meeting at Shadow Rock Park near Forsyth on September 20, 1980.

The tourism boom in Branson was both a blessing and a burden for WRVEC.

Ironically, the gasoline shortages of the 1980s actually enhanced the tourism business in Branson as people sought vacation destinations closer to home. White River, along with other area businesses, organized a program offering visitors a tank of gas upon leaving Branson to help stimulate tourism during a sluggish economy.

This pattern was to repeat again in the 1990s, with unprecedented growth and a recession that once again brought vacationers to the centrally located Branson. This time, the growth rate was so explosive both Chris Hamon and Larry Frazier observed had there not been another electric power provider in the area, the challenge of keeping pace with the growth might have been overwhelming. The co-op's two-year plans and long-range plans were amended repeatedly each time another loan application became necessary to keep pace with construction demands. Between 1975 and 1999, Larry Frazier steered the co-op through the massive growth that saw the co-op go from 13,000 to 42,000 meters. "The thing I am proudest of," he said, "was the quality of people I hired. I think I left the Co-op in very good hands."

General Manager Larry Frazier with the White River Board of Directors, 1981.

High Tech Answers

Among the people to whom Larry Frazier entrusted White River is current CEO Chris Hamon who began his career as an assistant engineer in October 1985. A native of the Tri-Lakes area, Chris grew up in Kirbyville and in 1984 earned his bachelor of science degree in electrical engineering at the University of Missouri. For a number of years, Chris

taught linemen training and is very proud of White River's up-to-date, OSHA-trained linemen. In 1989 he earned the designation of professional engineer (P.E.) while working his way up the corporate ladder at White River. On January 1, 1999, he was named CEO.

Though he is passionate about White River's people and their history, his focus is squarely on the co-op's future and is credited with taking the co-op into the technology age. "I requested the first personal computer in the building twenty-five years ago," he recalled. "Now we've even got PC's in everyone's truck, not just for communication but for identifying outages.

Long-time board members Glenn Harnden and Oscar Skaggs enjoy visiting with the members.

From a 1958 *Hill and Holler News*... What is a Member?

A member is the most important person in our business.

A member is not dependent on us; we are dependent on him.

A member is not an interruption in our work; he is the purpose of it.

A member is part of our business, not an outsider.

A member does us a favor when he calls.

A member is not a cold statistic; he is a human being with feelings.

A member is not someone to argue or match wits with.

A member deserves courteous treatment.

It's cut our outage time tremendously."

Under his leadership, White River implemented GIS, a geospatial mapping system, and AMR, an automated meter reading capability. Going one step further, White River then built an interface between these technologies that allowed the co-op to select and view outages graphically, determining outages down to the meter.

Linemen had to remove twisted metal from the lines when a tornado hit McCracken in Christian County, October 1984.

Then in 2009, Chris Hamon proudly reported that White River was one of eight utilities worldwide chosen by Google to implement the PowerMeter, a free electricity usage-monitoring tool that provides members with information on how much energy their homes are consuming. As part of the U.S. Department of Energy's initiative to promote the development of "smart grids," White River's automated meter reading technology is designed for accurate and efficient meter reading. These systems also help manage outages more effectively and can help reroute power around problem areas. Eventually, it will help members manage their energy costs by targeting their usage during the most cost efficient times of the day.

Rob Dalton, Jeff Pardek, and Doug Mann sporting co-op shirts at the 1997 annual meeting.

Layne Morrill

Layne Morrill, White River's longest serving board member, grew up two miles outside Reeds Spring and remembers well living without electricity. When his family's home was electrified in 1947, even though they only had one bulb in one room, Layne recalled, "It was certainly nice to have that one bulb!"

Layne's great-grandfather homesteaded in the area in 1893 and was the postmaster depicted in *The Shepherd of the Hills*. He still owns the property where the post office was located and with his deep roots, to him serving on the board is a simple matter of civic duty.

When he was first elected to the board in 1976, he was the only representative from Stone County, the smallest area at the time and now the second largest in the White River Valley. Layne has served as board secretary since 1979 and also served on the boards of KAMO Electric Power, Associated Electric, and the Consumer-Owned Energy Foundation. He has traveled the country helping cooperative boards raise pac funding at the local, state, and national levels. In 2006, the Table Rock Lake Area Chamber of Commerce presented Layne with its Community Service Award. On October 20, 2008, at the annual meeting of the Association of Missouri Electric Cooperatives held in Kansas City, Layne was honored with the Franklin R. Stork Democracy Award for his work on behalf of Missouri's electric cooperatives.

By partnering with the local business community, White River has set up a network of what Chris calls "interruptible consumers." These fifty-two member/consumers have stand-by generators that boost the co-op's distribution capabilities during peak demand. Chris estimates this network has saved the co-op approximately three million dollars a year over the last twenty years and saved local businesses from downtime they might otherwise have incurred without the reliable back-up power source.

Because of innovations like these, Chris Hamon was given the 2009 J. C. Brown CEO Communication Leadership Award through the electric co-op industry's Spotlight on Excellence Awards program. Citing Chris for his exceptional "inclusive method of strategic planning and attention to communication," the award was presented during the annual conference held for chief executives and general managers by the National Rural Electric Cooperative Association.

Ladies prepare for the members' arrival at the 1986 annual meeting. Betty Johnson is on the left, Alta Mae Cary is in the back.

Delbert Moore, Tom Alexander, and Ted Bookout prepare to hand out free lightbulbs, 1986.

Energy and the Environment

By 2000, sixty-five years since President Roosevelt signed the legislation creating the Rural Electrification Act, the issues surrounding electrical energy focused less on its generation and distribution and more on its impact on the environment. The phrase "global warming" made its way into the worldwide consciousness as energy and its impact on the environment became a politically charged issue.

Despite environmental concerns, demand for electricity remained on the rise. The Annual Energy Outlook released by the Energy Information Administration in 2004 showed residential energy use was projected to increase 25 percent by 2025. The future of rural electric cooperatives across the country would be determined by their ability to continue providing affordable electricity while addressing environmental concerns and the resulting legislation and regulations.

You'd better get there early or the doughnuts will be gone!

WRVEC's new Ozark office was built in 1986.

Lorraine Eiserman wields a mallet to help raise the tent for the 1988 annual meeting while Alta Mae Cary, Carol Campbell, Myrtle Booth, Shirley Albright, Bonnie Manson, and Brenda Wood keep a safe distance.

White River launched a number of initiatives and projects to proactively address both energy and environmental concerns. In 2004, they created a voluntary Green Power Program allowing members to purchase electricity in 100-kilowatt-hour blocks at a rate of $3.50 per block. Though the power purchased under this program does not actually flow from the renewable source directly to the member's meter, the energy purchased under the program was pooled with other participants with White River's generation and transmission (G & T), Associated Electric Cooperative, and provides the energy conscious consumer an opportunity to support such measures.

The Department of Agriculture Reorganization Act of 1994 expanded the REA's service to

The costumes may be glitzier these days, but country-western entertainment remains a favorite at the annual meetings.

include the building of infrastructure, like water and sewer service, in order to stimulate economic development in rural areas, and in April of 1995 the REA changed its name to the Rural Utilities Service. When WRVEC opened the Stone County Service Center on Highway 413 in Reeds Spring on May 17, 2004, it included the offices of White River Valley Environmental Services to address concerns over dysfunctional and abandoned septic tanks in Stone County. The building's infrastructure includes the AdvanTEx system, a high-tech alternative wastewater system that circulates the building's wastewater through a filtering system that cleans it and then uses it to irrigate the landscaping around the service center. The alternative systems are made available for purchase throughout the WRVEC area, in part to protect the cleanliness of Table Rock Lake. The Stone County Service Center also houses office clerks, line crews, and operations management providing improved response times for members in that area, particularly during storm-related outages.

Larry Frazier welcomes members to the 1988 annual meeting. Behind him are directors Joe Adams, Leslie Griffith, Oscar Skaggs, Howard Wade, George Simpson, Jim Hickman, Glenn Harnden, and Roy Matthews.

Dobie Youngblood and Delbert Moore celebrating his retirement, 1989.

WRVEC encouraged members to have their voices heard during the "Our Energy, Our Future" campaign.

Our Energy, Our Future

Between 2005 and 2008, electric bills across the country increased an average of 30 percent, largely because of increased environmental regulations and rising costs for coal, natural gas, and construction materials. Consumers in the coal-reliant Midwest were expected to experience a larger cost impact from the proposed carbon dioxide regulations.

In response to legislative trends, electric cooperatives across the country began working together to advocate for legislation that would be fair to rural cooperative members. A grassroots effort entitled, "Our Energy, Our Future: A Dialogue with America," arose encouraging co-op members to contact their legislators urging them to consider the rural co-ops when forming new regulations and creating legislation addressing climate change issues.

At White River, Jeff Pardeck, manager of member services, and Amy Rosier, communications coordinator, developed the local grassroots campaign. With the same can-do spirit the people of White River Valley displayed so many years ago, members responded in record numbers. They told their stories on print, video, and broadcast media about hardships that were likely to occur both to individuals and businesses if stringent climate change legislation was adopted. More than 114,000 messages, far beyond their goal of 50,000, were sent to Congress from White River members.

The present Ava office was built in 2006.

The New Branson Office

In July of 2009, WRVEC announced its decision to rebuild its headquarters. The existing building, dated from 1975, was very inefficient and in need of major repairs and system upgrades. The new building represents White River's proactive stance as a leading proponent of energy efficiency.

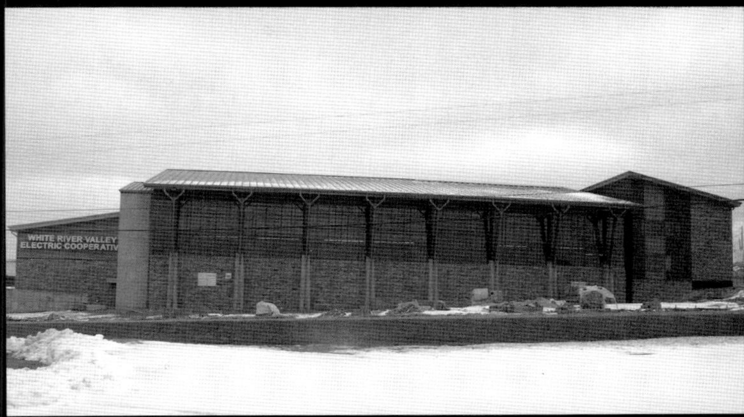

In addition to energy concerns, mandates resulting from the Homeland Security Act led to improved security measures intended to protect the new headquarters' dispatch area and focus on preventing identity theft.

The period of economic downturn preceding the decision meant that material and labor costs, as well as interest rates, were at an all-time low, making it the perfect time for the new facility.

Roy Clark, one of the biggest names to grace the annual meeting stage, performed in 2009.

On May 11, 2010, at the CONNECT '10 Conference of the NRECA, White River received the Edgar F. Chesnutt Award for Best Total Communication Program, the highest honor bestowed through the Spotlight on Excellence Awards program.

Though it will be decades before the challenges surrounding the supply of clean, renewable, and affordable energy are resolved, Chris Hamon summed up White River sentiments in the May 2009 *Current Times*: "Investments in renewable energy must be made with the impact on the end user's electric bill in mind. At WRVEC we support national energy and climate change legislation that can be sustained politically and economically over the decades."

Chris Hamon takes care to greet members as they arrive at the annual meetings and answers all their questions.

In 2009 Chris Hamon received the J. C. Brown CEO Leadership Award for his communication efforts.

White River's Community Commitment

Back in 1993, then general manager Larry Frazier launched Operation Round Up (ORU) out of his sincere concern for the people who make up the White River community. Through Operation Round Up, WRVEC members who wished to participate could have their electric bills rounded up to the next dollar each month. The extra monies then go to the WRVEC Trust made up of ten volunteer community leaders from the five-county area who dispense it to local organizations and needy families. As of April 2011—the eighteenth anniversary of the program—over three million dollars worth of assistance has been given to families and various community-based organizations through the generosity of White River's members.

ORU monies are also combined with proceeds raised through the Energy and Education Pro-Am and the Hooked on Education fishing tournaments. Proceeds from the tournaments benefit local children's charities and the White River Valley Electric Trust Scholarship Fund for local students. Over $1.1 million in college scholarships have been awarded.

When a crippling ice storm hit southwest Missouri in January of 2009, White River crews answered the call for help.

Every year since 2002, a team from WRVEC has participated in the Relay For Life to raise money for cancer patients. Additionally, donations from White River Valley Electric Cooperative help sustain food pantries and community outreach programs throughout the area. In October of 2009, ORU teamed up with the Conservation Federation of Missouri by reimbursing area meat processors who participated in the Share the Harvest program that allows hunters to donate some or all of their bounty. Over 1.9 million pounds of venison have been donated since the program's inception.

WRVEC participates in the annual Relay For Life.

A Solid Future Amid the Change

Whatever challenges the future holds the people of WRVEC stand poised to meet them with a balance of tradition and innovation. The annual meetings, though they've changed from the original festival-like gatherings under the big top, remain important avenues for communication with the members. Like those who came before, Chris Hamon continues the policy of having an "open door" for both employees and members, greeting members as they arrive at the annual meetings and answering their questions concerning equipment, wholesale power costs, and the uncertain future of energy regulations.

Today's annual meetings still have the festival feeling with lots of family activities. Inside, however, the latest technology helps communicate serious energy issues to the members.

A great deal has changed since White River's earliest days and while it is easy to give in to nostalgia, the reality is that life was much more difficult for many people back then. The people of WRVEC have done a great job of holding onto the best of their traditions while meeting the challenges of the modern world. The board of directors is no longer made up entirely of local farmers but now includes business owners, realtors, and investment bankers. At one time, the co-op built lines at no charge. Nowadays, with both businesses and people being more transient than in years past, they charge an up-front fee for building an electrical system. Despite the fact that underground lines cost four to five times more than overhead lines, people continue to request them, though as Chris says, "I'm not going to let their service put the rest of our members' service at risk."

Reliability of service plays a more important role than it did back when folks were far less dependent on electricity. As a cooperative instead of an

We Will Stomp You! White River's three-time defending champion Hollister Grape and Fall Festival Grape Stomp team celebrates after the 2009 competition. Back row: Dianne Rankin, Brian Rankin, Lynne Campbell, Heather Maring, Vanessa Jacoby, Adam Boyce, Amy Rosier, Chris Sidfrid, Diana Bradford, Justin Gage, Trisha Menzies, and Cami Stottle. Front row: Dylan Royston, Seth McCarter, Meagan Sidfrid, Rylea Call, and Allison Call.

White River's Board of Directors at the 2010 annual meeting. Seated: Joe Brazeale, Bill Cook, and George Simpson. Standing: CEO Chris Hamon, Russell Loftin, Russell Jackson, Keet Short, Bob Simmons, Pat Funk, Layne Morrill, Attorney David Smith, and Dobie Youngblood.

investor owned company, White River is free to focus on reliability to protect the continuity of its members' service. As always, cost remains a constant concern, particularly in the current economic downturn. In days past, the more electricity a member used, the cheaper their rate. But with increased generation costs, while some cooperatives in other states are charging high-use members a higher rate as a conservation measure, White River charges a constant rate, regardless of use. This happy medium echoes the phrase Chris has used on many occasions to illustrate White River's philosophy: "We're all in this together."

More than seventy years since its formation, WRVEC now has 5,412 miles of energized line, serves about 50,000 meters and approximately 43,000 members in its five-county area. One thing that has remained constant is today's WRVEC employees bring the same sense of mission to their work that the founders brought to those early schoolhouse and town hall meetings—a commitment to bringing a better life to the people of the White River Valley.

Index

About the Author

Pat Swinger began writing for the Donning Company Publishers after working with them to publish her hometown's history during its sesquicentennial in 2006. Pat raised her family in a suburb of St. Louis, during which time she received her degree from Washington University in St. Louis, and then returned to her hometown of O'Fallon, Missouri, in 1996. Since then she has been deeply involved in preserving local history, writing numerous newspaper articles and missives. Because of her abiding passion for local history, she enjoys working with organizations and corporations, helping them to preserve and tell their own stories.

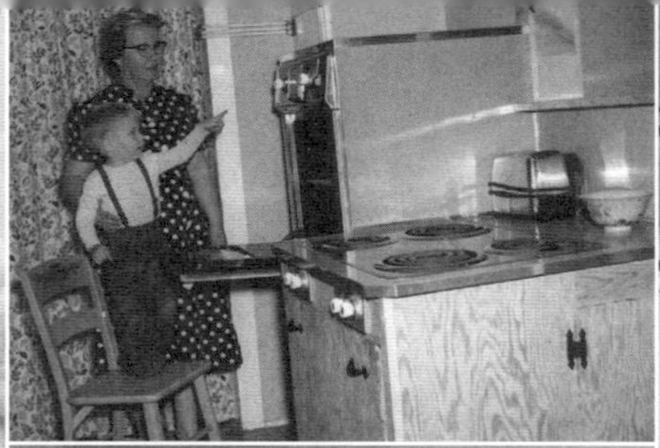

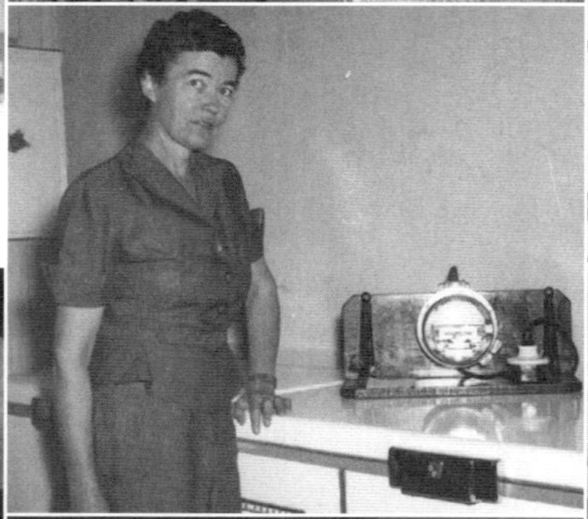